A FOXING LIFE

With Gun and Rifle

MIKE POWELL

To the fair countryside of Devon and its foxes
– it is impossible to quantify just how
much both have given me

AUTHOR
Mike Powell

DESIGN
Geraldine Chorley

EDITOR
Peter Carr

DEPUTY EDITOR
Colin Fallon

COVER PHOTOGRAPH
Shutterstock

PHOTOGRAPHY
Unless otherwise stated, photography is courtesy of Mike Powell,
Brian Phipps, Shutterstock or iStock.

British Library Cataloguing-in-Publication Data
A catalogue record for this book is available from the British
Library

ISBN 978-0-9549597-4-6

Printed in England by Polestar Wheatons

Blaze Publishing Ltd
Lawrence House, Morrell Street, Leamington Spa, Warwickshire
CV32 5SZ
T: 01926 339808   F: 01926 470400
E: info@blazepublishing.co.uk W: www.blazepublishing.co.uk

CONTENTS

FOREWORD

It was a long time before I actually met Mike Powell in person. Mike and I were two of the *Sporting Rifle* originals. In fact it's a sobering thought, but we are the two remaining scribes left from when *Sporting Rifle* morphed from the supplement it first was inside *Target Sports* into the standalone title it is today. I was Yorkshire-based back then and Mike was firmly rooted in deepest Devon, so the likelihood of us crossing paths was remote. At the time I was just getting used to this thing called the internet, and Mike was my first 'ether' colleague, one who I wouldn't actually meet in person for five years.

Our editor in those halcyon days was the redoubtable and quite, quite, mad Charlie Jacoby, who none of us could ever get hold of on the phone. Indeed we only heard from CJ two days before print date. It was a recurring monthly miracle that the magazine actually went out on time, but it always did despite our concerns. Charlie's catchphrase whenever we questioned the content of our own copy was always the same: "That'll do, perfect" – but the copy had always been 'Charlified' come the day our magazine arrived.

Mike was the number one foxing scribe back then, and he still is now, which is a great testament to his knowledge and writing skills. When I eventually took on the editor's reins from Charlie, Mike Powell was the first to congratulate me, and he was always a source of encouragement in my first few issues after I had jumped in at the deep end. I shall long remember and be ever grateful for Mike's support at the beginning of my editorship, especially when CJ's mobile went straight to answerphone mid-crisis – I quickly learnt that CJ's 'consultant editor' role was an honorary rather than a working title.

As far as foxing goes, Mike Powell is one of the most knowledgeable experts in his field that I have ever had the privilege to work with. There are many efficient fox shooters operating today, but Mike Powell is the full deal and there isn't a method of control he hasn't or isn't willing to try within the realms of the law. As restrictive as the current regulations are, Mike consistently does the job and returns home with the errant fox or foxes, and this book will help you do the same.

What I have always found fascinating about Mike is his complete admiration and respect for his vulpine quarry. As a fox controller, he goes to great pains to target the marauding animal rather than just killing every fox out of hand. Don't get me wrong – as a keeper, Mike's shoot was a very dangerous place for a fox to tread, and he showed them no mercy. But in areas without any gamebird or specific wildlife concerns, Mike is happy to let the fox go about its business and take its rightful place in contemporary British flora and fauna.

This book has been a long time coming. Mike has spent a life time in pursuit of the fox with gun, rifle and other engines of destruction. Some of the methods are now outdated, but they nevertheless give an interesting background to how lessons learned back in the old days have shaped Mike's perception and approach to vermin control today.

There can be little doubt the author has lived life to the full in our green and pleasant land. He knew when to take advantage of nature's bounty even from an early age, but Mike has always endeavoured to keep the balance. He was part and parcel of the post-war countryside, and as agricultural and gamebird husbandry developed in the wake of the Second World War, so did he to the present day.

It is easy to forget that Mike has lived seven decades when you are in his company. He still retains the enthusiasm of a fresh-faced 16-year-old, and has a mischievous wit about him that many professional comics would swap a kidney for – trust me, I have been at the receiving end of it on many an occasion.

There is little doubt in my mind, and the minds of most others who regularly read Mike's articles, that his greatest skill is wielding the pen, and transferring his vast knowledge to the page. Mike often makes the point that the fox rarely does what you first expect it to, but with a little forethought and applied dedication, vulpine cunning can be overcome. Glean everything you can from this book, always strive to be the best shot – your quarry deserves nothing less – and above all be safe. Our continued sport depends on it. Keep the faith.

Peter Carr
Editor-in-chief, Sporting Rifle magazine

FOXING: THE EARLY YEARS

Like many others, I came into shooting largely by chance. It was mainly because my family lived in a rural part of Devon among the red soil hills and green fields, in a place where life in the 1940s was very much as it had been for generations. The countryside had been left more or less untouched by the ravages of war, and for a small boy who loved to be out on his own among the woods and fields, it was a paradise. A lad could roam untroubled by the happenings that fill our lives today.

Those days have, in the main, disappeared – sadly for good, I suspect. Trust in those who walked the fields by day and night has all but gone. But back then, violence was totally unknown, and the people I met treated me well. I was allowed to roam at will over large areas of the land, usually with an air rifle, and as I got older I tried to help out a bit at harvest. The sight of the fields being opened up with scythes and the clatter of the binder are but distant memories, as are the sight of all the farm workers, dogs and boys waiting as the binder completed the last few rounds and the hordes of rabbits broke for cover.

Landowners were, almost without exception, happy to have a lad around, provided he did what he was told. It was years until I saw my first tractor – all the work was done by horses, and giants they were to me. When I was launched onto those broad brown backs, I felt like I ruled the world.

The collies were masters at working with the binder and would account for dozens of rabbits; I would go home having been given a couple, feeling tired but happy. That was the way the countryside was and I have little doubt that there are still a few similar places like that in the more remote parts of the country.

This was the backdrop that marked the way I would travel over the next 70-odd years. Even now I look back with huge feelings of nostalgia for those happy, long days spent largely on my own or in the company of good country people. Those among you who were privileged enough to start your lives in that sort of world will know exactly what I mean.

My first years were spent in very different surroundings from those I would encounter during the rest of my life. I suppose Wembley, in what was then Middlesex, was as far removed from Teignmouth in Devon, where most of the maternal side of the family hailed from, as it could be. Circumstances during the war dictated a move back to Devon, and it was here, over 70 years ago, that I came to the countryside that would dominate the rest of my life.

Arriving, we took up residence on the outskirts of the small seaside town in an old toll house that was surrounded by fields and small woods. About a mile up the hill were the fringes of the Haldon Hills, which are now renowned for their substantial population of fallow deer. Those days spent surrounded by farmland and with distant views of the sea presented me, a small boy,

with a veritable wonderland just waiting to be explored.

Let it be said now that neither of my parents were what could be termed 'country folk'. My father was clerk to the local district council and my mother was just that, a mother and housewife. We also shared the house with the local gravedigger. A tall, gaunt man who during the winter months suffered the most appalling chaps on his hands after digging graves by hand in the wet and cold – but never once did I hear him complain. He also stuck in my memory by having the dubious ability to clear his plate of virtually everything on it. I am sure he drew the line at chop bones, but anything in the way of fish bones, including the back bones of cod and haddock, were all dealt with by a fascinatingly ill-fitting pair of false teeth. This daunting figure had three sons, two of whom had served in the war and were recently demobbed, and the youngest that still lived with us. He was a godlike figure to me for one reason, and that was that he had an air rifle.

This wondrous item was kept in a cupboard under the stairs, and whenever there was nobody about, I would open the door and gaze in wonder at it – never, of course, actually touching it. This went on for quite a while before I actually plucked up the courage to ask if I could see it. Fred, the son, who was always good to me, took the rifle into the garden, put a few flower pots out as targets, and proceeded to hit them with monotonous regularity, suitably impressing the very impressionable small boy.

The rifle itself was a BSA underlever, which of course was miles too big for a nine-year-old. However, not wishing for a second to let a chance like this pass, I soon learned I could fire it after a fashion by putting the stock either over my shoulder or under my arm. Neither system was conducive to accuracy, but I was able to fire it in the general direction of the flower pots. Cocking it was a problem, but by resting the butt on the ground and putting all my young muscles to work, I could actually get it to cock. It was a bit dodgy by present-day standards, but back then we just did what we did with precious little thought as to the consequences.

Shortly after this first adventure with the air rifle under the somewhat cavalier guidance of Fred, I was told I could help myself to it whenever I wanted. Remember, this was a very long time ago and we lived well away from anyone, so I was free to roam pretty much anywhere I wanted.

Farmers then seemed happy enough to let me go on their ground. I suspect they couldn't really see such a small boy being a problem. My first kill, to my eternal shame, was a blue tit, and I can picture the whole episode as if it were yesterday. I will not go into the details, but at the time I was over the moon with excitement – though even at that age I thought it better not to say anything to my parents.

Time passed, and the long summer holidays were spent trailing round after the farm worker on the next-door farm, a kindly man called Tom Farley. Tom, who had a couple of children of his own, took me under his wing and taught me about catching rabbits. In those days there were countless numbers of these pests around my home, and the damage they caused had to be seen to be believed. Great areas of all the cereal crops were devastated. They even ravaged the oats, a crop rabbits usually tend to ignore – so great were their numbers that they were glad to feed on anything that presented itself.

The usual method of catching in those days was by snare or the now illegal gin trap. I still have a couple of these as mementoes of those days, and looking at them now,

I have to admit what cruel engines they were. However, this never even crossed my young mind, and with Tom's expert tuition I became pretty good at setting them. The usual place was in the entrance to the countless holes that perforated every hedge on the farm. With a trowel I would dig a trench just deep enough to house the jaws and spring, allowing enough depth to cover everything with a layer of sieved soil. Setting them in the mouth of the buries not only produced results, but it also gave a measure of protection from the buzzards and foxes that found the trapped rabbits an easy source of food. If, however, the traps were placed close to the hole, the luckless rabbit would get inside as far as it could and would most times be overlooked by the predators.

Another method was to take advantage of the rabbit's natural instinct to investigate freshly revealed soil. Cutting a turf about 18 inches square and setting the gin in the soil would almost invariably result in a catch. More often than not it would be a buck. Why, I never really knew – possibly they were bolder and investigated new soil faster than the more timid does.

I found setting the snares took more experience and skill than the gin. Tom pointed out the runs and where to place the snare – right in the middle of the pad or landing spot. The biggest snag was the fact that you had to be up very early to get the rabbits before the predators got there first. The biggest pests were the buzzards. They were everywhere – this was long before their disappearance owing to, in the main, the chemical DDT, which was widely used in agriculture. I believe one of the effects it had was to cause sterility. Nowadays, of course, such poisons have been banned, and the buzzard is swiftly returning to its immediate post-war numbers.

To me, getting up at first light was never a problem, and the excitement of following the trap line never waned. Tom and I caught countless rabbits by using gins and snares, but eventually the former were banned, much to the dismay of the farming community. Certainly I can understand their concerns as there were truly huge numbers of rabbits, and although undoubtedly cruel, the traps did their job very well. As one does when things of great

Mike at age 11, his trousers ripped from chasing a lost ferret

Above left: 'Dad's trying to look like a hunter!'
Above right: The view from Mike's childhood home looking across to Dartmoor

importance happen to you when you are young, you remember them with great clarity, and my very first snared rabbit was one such memory.

Tom had been giving me lessons on snaring and I was determined to 'go solo'. Removing one of his snares, I searched for a good place to set it. In the lane just up the road from where I lived was a typical Devon lane. The steep banks towered above my young head so I was limited as to where I could till my misappropriated snare. I found a run under an ash root where rabbits had clearly been travelling. Tying the cord to another handy root, I set the tealer peg so the loop of the snare was about an inch away from the lower side of the root covering the run, and a fraction smaller than the run itself.

Next morning I did my trap round as usual, leaving my own private-enterprise effort till last. To my great excitement there was a dead rabbit suspended, cleanly caught

round the neck and as dead as a doornail. With my very first rabbit caught in a snare, I was a happy lad for sure. Strangely enough, I still pass this lane fairly regularly, and although the hedges don't seem nearly as high and the rabbits have long gone, the memories are as sharp as ever.

Time passed quickly and I became more and more immersed in the countryside around my home. School was, to me, a complete waste of time. There were so many more important things to do with my time than spend it behind a desk. I did reasonably well at primary school, even passing the 11-plus first time, but what really caused me problems was my introduction to the world of the ferret.

For some time I had seen some decidedly rough-looking characters in the fields close to home. They were usually there on a weekend, but also on the odd weekday there would be two or three of them. Watching them from a safe distance, I could see they were doing something in the hedges, often spending considerable lengths of time just standing around. They really intrigued me, and it wasn't long before I asked my mentor Tom what they were doing. "Ferreting," he said. At that time I had no idea what a ferret was or what you did with it when you had one. More explanations followed, and once I learned that these 'ferrets' helped you catch rabbits I couldn't wait to find out more. Whenever I saw the dodgy-looking men in the field I would go and watch them, never getting closer than about 100 yards as they did look a bit fierce. Once or twice they called me over, but at little more than 10 years old, I found this too big a step to take. Tom assured me they were harmless, but although I was truly desperate to see what went on I was never brave enough to take that final step.

This state of affairs went on for a couple of months in the run up to Christmas 1947. Things were a bit tight in those post-war years and I never expected much in the way of presents, but Christmas day passed happily with the usual festive fare and a few things in the stocking. I was also told there was going to be a bit of a treat the following day. I was deeply suspicious – these 'treats' often turned out to be a long walk with Mum and Dad. The next morning I was told to dress up in my old clothes as I was going out. I was right, then – the dreaded walk loomed.

There was then a knock on the door, and there was Tom and with him the three men from the fields! Mum gave me a canvas bag with some string things inside, which I really didn't have a clue about – they looked singularly unexciting. I was introduced to the three, who wasted no time in saying, "Come on then boy, we'll try and get a rabbit or two."

As I remember it, we only caught a few but I was in heaven. In a few hours I had

learnt what a ferret was, learnt what the string things in the bag were for, and seen my first rabbit bolt into one of them (the nets). My world really changed from then on. Delivered me home clutching one of the rabbits, I declared that that was what I was

New game: The author outside the 'pre-fab' with his first pheasant

going to be when I grew up: a rabbit catcher! I have to say my parents, although never standing in my way, never seemed too keen on my choice of future career. As well as the rabbit catcher idea, at various stages I also professed a desire to be a slaughterman and a gamekeeper. Looking back, I suspect that to a clerk at the local council and his home-loving wife, these ideas seemed fairly horrific.

For the next year when the ferreting season arrived, I would blatantly play truant on any day the men were ferreting. I have no recollection what my parents thought but that didn't matter – I just had to be out there.

After a couple of years we left the gravedigger's house and moved into one of the pre-fabricated bungalows that were springing up all over the country and were designed to house those folk who had lost their homes during the war. Fortunately for me, ours was situated on the other side of Teignmouth, right on the outskirts of the

Ferret frenzy: The ferreting bug bit early for Mike

town and bordered again with field. On top of that it was only half a mile from the local refuse tip – more of that later.

By now I had moved to the local grammar school, which was to prove a bit of a disaster educationally. I was more than able to hold my own at school but my heart was never in it – I only wanted to be out in my beloved fields. The only good thing that came out of school was that in my form was a lad called Johnny who had exactly the same interests as me. Throughout our school life we became close friends and spent vast amounts of time ratting, rabbiting, lamping and increasing our knowledge of the countryside around us. He moved away in due course, but we still meet up and remember the good times when we were lads in a different world.

My original mentors were out of reach as neither I nor my parents had any means of transport. But by now I had, through the good offices of my father, teamed up with a couple of chaps who lived near me who went ferreting. Big Sid and Old Charlie were keen ferreters, and had bought the rabbiting rights on most of the farmland around us. This was a common practice then as there was a ready market for both rabbits and their skins – I never knew the actual finances but I do know that Sid was keen to catch every rabbit there was. To this end he was a hard man to please. He was, to me, huge. He worked on the local docks and at some point had come into contact with a crane hook, which had given him a severe head wound and left him with a huge scar and a damaged eye. This gave him a somewhat scary aspect. He was, however, a gentle giant, and I really took to him despite learning several new words, particularly when I inadvertently overlooked a bolt hole or when a rabbit escaped the net before I could get a hand on it.

Charlie on the other hand, although he appeared very old to me at my tender age, was a bit of a lad. Long retired, he would encourage me to skip school so we could go on 'secret' rabbiting missions. These were mostly on land we had the rights to, although looking back, I think more often than not the old man and the boy ended up in places that weren't 'ours'. Everything we caught Charlie would sell, and we would split the proceeds.

After one particularly good outing, this time on 'our' land, we struggled home with a couple of dozen decent rabbits. This was yet another midweek effort, and the following weekend Sid decided we would try a couple of hedges where he knew there were plenty of rabbits. Unfortunately it was the same hedge Charlie and I had ferreted midweek. We always walked to the land we were rabbiting – sometimes this would be a couple of miles away, as was this patch. Naturally I kept quiet and waited to see what happened; it wasn't long before Sid started muttering how

some poaching so-and-so had been there, and if he caught them there would be hell to pay. I have a feeling he suspected old Charlie, but there was no way Charlie was saying anything, so we moved on. Charlie and I had many adventures together, most of them just on the brink of legality, but I learnt a lot from the old man and missed him when he passed away.

Although there were foxes around, I never really paid much attention to them in the beginning. The farms were predominately dairy, and to be honest most farmers were more than happy to see foxes as a means of helping stem the ever-increasing tide of rabbits. They only became a nuisance when they started removing rabbits from the snare and gin.

The first fox I ever saw killed was one early winter's morning when we were setting off for a day's ferreting, crossing a rough field covered in frost. A fox jumped in front of us and was off. Our lurcher Prince was after it like a flash, and after a long and testing run, brought it down. By the time we reached it, it was dead. It seemed very large to me after the rabbits. Charlie boned out the brush with a couple of hazel sticks and presented it to me, and that was it – I was hooked. While I still relentlessly pursued rabbits, fox was definitely top of the list of quarry species.

By now I was into my teens and every spare moment was spent out in the fields. I had also graduated to a shotgun, but I have to say that my skills both with gun and rifle owe a lot to spending the preceding years with air rifles, starting as previously mentioned with a BSA underlever and then with a BSA Cadet, which my grandmother bought me when I was 11. The memorable first shot with that little rifle was spot on. It hit the cotton reel I had hung from the fence, ricocheted straight back and cracked the window in the 'prefab'. I was more than

happy at scoring a hit first off; my parents took a slightly different view.

Rabbits and rats featured highly on the programme, particularly as by now we were living close to the local refuse tip. Vast numbers of rats lived among the piles of waste in those pre-poison days, and I spent countless hours with the air rifles shooting huge numbers. It was excellent and rewarding sport, which even today I still enjoy, although the numbers are nothing like they were.

Bear in mind we were still living, by present-day standards, in the dark ages. No television, only a battery-powered radio (which I never listened to anyway), and the internet was, like travel to the moon, never in a boy's mind, so everything had to be learned from scratch. Books on shooting were expensive and we had little money, so whatever I wanted to do in the way of trapping and shooting, certain things was self taught.

I made many errors along the way – back then I knew little about calibres, shot sizes, rifle makes and so on – but before long I became old enough to buy my first real firearm. This was a BSA Sportsman Five. Why I ended up with that I have no idea – probably it was all there was in the shop. This came with open sights, which in due course I changed to aperture. I practised on my rat friends until I became pretty accurate; it was at this point my affair with the fox really began.

Waiting out one night among the debris left by the dustcarts, I noticed a fox working its way towards me some two or three hundred yards away. As the smell of the tip would undoubtedly cover the scent of even a rather smelly youth, I decided to keep still and see what happened next. Even now when I read of the so-called 'buck fever' I can't help going back to that evening on the tip. I really thought I couldn't breathe

– my heart was pounding and my hands were trembling. This was the moment I had dreamed of for years. By now the fox was about 100 yards away and still coming, only pausing now and then to pick up a tasty morsel from that day's rubbish collection. It was the biggest fox I had ever seen – mind you, I hadn't seen many, and apart from the one the lurcher had killed, I had certainly never been this close to one. Still it came on – by now it was only 50 yards away. Summoning up what senses I had and desperately trying to stop shaking, I lined up the Parker Hale aperture rear sight with the hooded bead foresight just behind the fox's ear. To this day I remember how the

Above: Dad with a Greener GP 12-bore, Mike with a Cogswell side-by-side
Left: Mike's quarry of choice inevitably became the fox

wobble completely stopped me taking the shot. Not wishing to lose the opportunity, I lined up on the chest just behind the front leg. Even that substantial target seemed too small, but as by now the fox had realised that something was up and was showing signs of nervousness, I decided to shoot. At the shot, the fox spun round and for a moment I thought I had missed, but to my immense surprise, delight and amazement, after a couple of faltering steps it dropped. There on the town's refuse tip, my foxing career had taken off.

Living not far away was the local keeper. Ron was a good man, although I knew that he, in the way of keepers, didn't trust anyone who carried a gun of any sort. However, he was the only one I could go to, as my mother would have been horrified if I had come through the door with a dead fox.

Fortunately Ron was at home in his typical thatched cottage. When he saw I had a fox, his normally reserved attitude changed and I was ushered into his backyard.

He asked me what I was going to do with it. I hadn't even thought about that! "Skin it out, boy, and sell it," was his advice. I was good at skinning rabbits but had never tackled a fox. Hanging it up on a couple of s-hooks, Ron guided me through the process, right down to boning out the brush with a couple of hazel sticks just like old Charlie had used some years before. Next we stretched the skin out inside the barn door to dry. "Come back in a week," were my instructions, and so I did. Rolling it up and wrapping in brown paper, Ron gave me the address of Horace Friend in far off Wisbech, Cambridgeshire, who it appeared bought fox skins.

What to do with a dead fox? Back then, it had some use and monetary value

Having been assured I would be paid, I waited and checked the post on a daily basis. About 10 days later an envelope arrived for me. Inside was an invoice and a cheque for about £10! This was a fortune to me. The invoice said that it was a mid-quality winter pelt. I dealt with this firm for many, many years and always found them fair. Today I see the building in Wisbech is listed, though sadly there is no longer a trade in skins. This was one of the anti-shooting brigade's first successes as far as I know. It has always struck me as strange that people considered banning the sale of skins a way of protecting foxes. In those days they didn't become just another dead fox – they provided something that was of use.

Anyway, the arrival of that cheque was a life-changer for me. There and then I decided I could make some real money from fox skins. I already sold all the rabbit skins I got – together, of course, with the meat, which I either sold privately or to the local butchers.

I always saved the money I got from the sale of the skins. With that, I upgraded my exceedingly dodgy Belgian 12-bore hammer gun to a Luigi Franchi semi-automatic five-shot. We had been lamping rabbits for some time using, by present standards, some decidedly 'Heath Robinson' equipment. The first 'lamp' we ever used was a cardboard tube with five U2 batteries in it, wired up to one of our cycle lamps, the sort that when you screwed down the knob on top of it squeaked furiously. There were two main disadvantages with this piece of equipment: firstly, the beam it threw was

Doubling up: A right and a left with the old hammer 12-bore

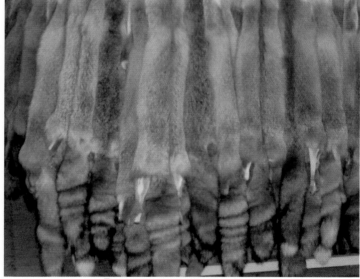

Fox pelts: Once a sought-after commodity, now made redundant by legislation

A trip to the local motorcycle dealers soon had an old but serviceable motorcycle headlamp in our possession. The next thing was power. To start with, we went down the route of using 6-volt second-hand motorcycle batteries. This was a massive step up from the cardboard tube, but still we needed more power. As I said before, there was no source of information so we really had to sort things out ourselves. Years later it transpired that the few people who were starting to lamp back then followed pretty much the same route, and without exception suffered the same problems.

Our eventual set-up was a couple of 12-volt wet acid car batteries wired up through a Woolworths switch to a car headlamp. Two batteries were needed, as when we were out all night one would invariably start to lose power so it was back to base for a changeover. Now our main problems were firstly that the switch gear invariably overheated if the lamp was kept on for more than a few minutes, and secondly the acid from the batteries rotted everything out extraordinarily quickly. The ex-army kit bags housing the battery would last a month if you were lucky, and jackets, trousers and everything else ended up with large holes burnt in them.

But we soldiered on and started to get results. The gun we used exclusively was the Luigi Franchi 12-bore five-shot semi-auto, the big advantage of that particular gun was that it could be used one-handed while holding the lamp in the other. It was totally reliable and it served me well for very many years until it was eventually stolen.

A typical night's foxing was somewhat different to how it would be today. To start with we had no transport except for our pushbikes, so two of us would set off at first dark and cycle to the clay pits where much of our shooting was done. A wild place full of rabbits, ponds and bramble,

only about 20 yards and very yellow, and secondly, if it was raining the cardboard tube got soggy and the batteries fell out. We did manage to shoot the odd rabbit, but soon realised that for foxes something far more powerful would be needed.

it was a haven for large numbers of foxes that moved out into the surrounding fields, which was where we would be. Early efforts brought more frustration than success, but we learned from our many mistakes. To start with we used Eley Maximum five shot as we thought these were the most powerful cartridges there were – Alphamax were just too expensive. However we soon learned that more foxes got away than were picked up, so we decided to load our own. After much experimentation with everything from 4s up to SG, we eventually settled on BBs as being the best for our use. I still use this shot size to this day.

A quick word on our reloading: we were using a lot of cartridges in those days, particularly on rabbits as there was no problem getting rid of shotgun-shot rabbits. We loaded with five shot for rabbit and BB for fox. We didn't know much about the dark art of loading, so it was a bit hit-and-miss to start with. I found loading paper cases relatively easy but encountered problems when the first plastic cases arrived on the scene. I had loaded about 50 of these new cases one night we were out after rabbits. As we moved quietly through the fields on a still night, we kept hearing this strange rustling noise, but for the life of us we couldn't trace it. We had several shots with little effect, which was strange as Johnny and I were getting pretty good with the guns. Eventually we tracked the strange noise to the gun and found that when it was carried barrel down, shot was running out of the cartridges as the crimp was opening up. It was a problem for a while, but I eventually cleared it by crimping much harder – at some point the plastic itself seemed to become more malleable.

I don't know when we first started calling foxes. It may have been thanks to my uncle, who lived in Canada and was a Mountie,

did a lot of hunting and sent me copies of Hunting and Shooting in Canada. These I read and reread, marvelling at tales of shooting bear, elk, moose and wolf. Heady stuff back then – I recall reading about guns with really exciting names like Ithaca, Savage and Ruger. There were, I think, articles where mention was made of calling foxes and coyotes by making a noise like a rabbit squealing. This set me thinking. My first mechanical call was the wheel from a Hornby train set carriage, as I remembered that when very small I had blown through a wheel that had come off its axle and it made a whistling noise. We also practised sucking on our grubby hands, producing the now well-known squeal.

Calling, as I shall discuss later, is an imprecise science. Today there are a vast range of calls of all sorts available – but back then it was very much learning by trial and error.

So what sort of success were we getting in those early days? It was a harsh learning curve. More hours than I care to remember were spent traipsing across the fields in pursuit of foxes, and there were many blank nights – remember we were using a shotgun, which had a range of, at best, 40 yards. The .22 rifle we found was just not up to the job – again, no scope, just aperture or open sights. We would probably be out five nights a week, and at best, in the beginning, finish the week with five or six foxes. The money we got for them was good by those days' standards, but above all we just loved what we were doing. I was starting to think that I could probably earn more from rabbits and foxes than from more conventional means, so I decided to give it a go. Another factor back then that affected lads of my age was National Service. Although it was the late fifties and we all knew that the two years' compulsory service in either the army, air force or – less

Nice wheels: With the acquisition of the Ariel 350, Mike's foxing world opened up

likely – the navy would come to an end, it was still almost inevitable I would be called up, so trying my hand at foxing for a living didn't seem much of a risk.

By now I was the proud owner of a motorcycle. Graduating from the inevitable BSA Bantam, I now had an Ariel 350, and my horizons opened up considerably. No longer would I have to cycle with a 12-volt battery and all the other gear hung precariously on a pushbike. I now had shooting rights over a large area of land and was out most nights during the week after rabbit and fox. During the day, ferreting and setting snares for both of the main quarry species took up a considerable amount of my time. I had kept ferrets from the early days with old Charlie, and in fact I still do. Ferreting is something you either love or hate. I have always enjoyed working and breeding ferrets, and at this time of my life they really prove their worth.

However, there was a looming black cloud on the horizon – one quite apart from the National Service one. The word was that there was a disease that affected rabbits starting up in France. Myxomatosis it was called, and to be honest we who were

involved in the countryside didn't make much of it at the time. Little did we realise what an impact it would have.

The foxing side was flourishing. Demand for skins was high and there was no shortage of them. Clearly they were of no use during the summer months as the pelts were pretty well worthless at that time of year, so they were left alone. This would gradually change as the years passed. By now, with constant practice, I was taking increasing numbers of foxes. Snaring played a large part in this – I had about 100 down at any one time. Results from this method vary considerably, and as with anything involved with foxes, nothing is guaranteed. Setting snares is an art, and although I have had reasonable success using this method, there are those who really have the knack. The best I ever came across was a local retired farmer – now he was good. He showed me his way of tilling a fox wire – but I never achieved the results he did. We did start up a rather good partnership, though – he would give me all the foxes he snared and I would skin them and send them off. We would then split the resulting profits. This system worked well until he became too old to get about.

One of the reasons most of our foxes were shot with a shotgun was because they usually caused less damage to the skin than a rifle bullet, the exception being the odd .22LR behind the ear. The pellet holes, we were told by the tanners, were easily concealed; of course the best were snared.

Skinning them became second nature. I would hang the fox up up by the back legs with the pelvic area about head height, and make a cut down the inside of each back leg, running down until it reached the front of the lower jaw. I then made two more incisions up the inside of each front leg and then I was ready to go. Depending on age and condition, some were easier than

Tilling a fox wire: An art that requires a lifetime's practice to perfect

covered in chrome accessories including aerials. I never quite worked out why a scooter needed an aerial, but it became the fashion to hang things on them including nylon fur imitation fox brushes. Now I knew someone (me) who had literally hundreds boxed up. Would the trendy mod brigade like some real fox brushes? You bet they would. I put an advert in the local paper offering them at 10 shillings each – 50p by modern standards. I sold the lot in one weekend.

Returning to the skinning process, after the skin was removed they would be stretched out on a board, usually plywood, and pinned all the way round, keeping the pins as close to the edge as possible. The board would then be placed in as airy a spot as possible and left to air dry.

I have to point out that I was still living at home and my parents were not exactly enthusiastic about my newfound career. I had run a couple of ideas past them about my future. One was being a slaughterman, the other a gamekeeper. I had spent some time at the local slaughterhouse as a lad helping out and really enjoyed it, But my parents, without ever actually saying no, made it abundantly clear that neither of these two professions were what they had envisioned for their son. Still, with National Service looming, no real decisions could be made.

The drying boards, therefore, were kept in the cellar. At times there were a lot. The smell of fox was ever-present, and looking back I can only wonder at the extreme patience my parents showed. I, too, constantly had the smell of fox about me, especially when mating time came round (the fox's, not mine). However, without a doubt the worst smell where dealing with animals was concerned came when I was skinning out a stoat. Unfortunately I nicked the scent gland at the rear end. Now

others; I much preferred to skin them warm as the pelt usually came away much easier then. Starting with the back legs, I would peel back the skin, first having made a cut around the 'elbow' joint. Care had to be taken when at the back of the legs, as parts of muscle and gland would be inclined to stick to the shin.

Once the back legs were out, lifting the skin from the back at the base of the tail enabled the brush to be boned out. Once this was done, the skin could be pulled right down to the chest area, where it had to be eased off the ribs and front legs. Further pulling brought it to the base of the ears, which were cut through and the rest of the skull skinned out. The whole process would take about 10 minutes, I would guess. Considerable care had to be taken not to cut the skin as this would cause a drop in price.

As years went by, for some reason the boned-out brush was no longer required, so I kept them. They dried out and were stored in cardboard boxes. I have no idea why I kept them but it certainly paid off years later. In the 1960s, in the era of mods and rockers, scooters were everywhere, Many will remember how they were that did stink – it was awful and lingered for a considerable time. I think that was the last stoat I ever skinned, and I certainly still have no wish to repeat the process.

Time in my late teens was passing very quickly – then myxomatosis arrived. We had heard reports that it was in Kent, and assumed it would take forever to arrive down here in Devon. How wrong we were. I was out after a particularly troublesome fox at a nearby village when I saw a rabbit crouched by the hedge. Bizarrely, it didn't move. By the time I got to it I could see what has now become an all too common sight: bulging, pus-filled eyes and a body visibly shrinking towards death. The disease was here.

It was August and by the middle of the month the fields smelled like nothing I had come across before. Dead and dying rabbits were everywhere. Crows, magpies and the rest bounced through the legions of the doomed, picking at them at will. In the end we would just go out with sticks, putting as many of them out of their misery as we could. It was truly awful. We heard estimates that it was about a 98 per cent mortality rate.

As we know, the disease has been with us from those days in the 1950s until now. In fact as I write this the foul scourge of myxi has reared its head yet again, to a much greater degree than before. Whether this is down to weather conditions, the wet summer of 2012 giving ideal breeding conditions for the blood-sucking insects that spread myxi, or whether there has been a change in the disease itself by natural or induced means, I have no idea. All I know is that nationwide, rabbit numbers are decreasing substantially.

When the disease first struck it certainly had an impact on fox numbers. The following year there were many large litters of cubs born, and while the abundance of

easy prey lasted, they thrived. I was taking, on average, about 400 foxes a year at that time, but then two things happened. First, fox numbers started to drop, and second, my National Service papers arrived. As with so many of us in those days, things would change forever.

THE LATER YEARS AND LAMPING TECHNOLOGY

Today I suspect a large percentage of foxes shot are killed with a rifle – in fact apart from the occasional chance shot presented when out pigeon or rabbit shooting, or on the game shoot where ground game is allowed, the numbers shot with guns is probably microscopic compared with the numbers killed with rifles. But back then, things were different, and here would be an appropriate place to describe the methods I employed when using a shotgun for foxes.

It was a rarity to wait out for a fox. Virtually all were spotted with a lamp – that was the easy bit, and the next thing was getting within 40 yards or less to ensure a clean kill. This was mainly achieved by calling, but as those who call foxes know, they don't always respond in the way you would like. More often than not they totally ignore your efforts, or worse, turn tail and disappear over the hill. So we had to resort to plan B and get out to them. Early efforts proved unsuccessful, but with time and practice and the necessity to make money, our efforts bore fruit.

I preferred to go out alone – it is one fewer person to make noise and produce scent

(back then, those factors were important – they matter much less today). If working as a pair, though, one would lamp and spot, and the other would have the gun. I preferred the five-shot semi-auto loaded with BBs. This did not damage the pelt to any degree, and was good out to about 50 yards. The lamps and battery were the set-up I described in the first chapter.

We had a lot of cliff land that held a large number of foxes, and by Devon standards the fields were large. Normally we would walk all night, starting at about 9pm and going on until it got too light. Keeping close to the hedges, we would scan the lamp briefly across the field we were in, and eventually would spot a pair of eyes. This was sheep country, and they were everywhere. But it was not long before you could differentiate between sheep and fox – probably just as well. This problem was nowhere near as great as it is today, when rifles are used at long range and there is always the possibility of a mistake. We had to get close, so identification was easy.

With Charlie spotted, our next move very much depended on how the fox reacted to

Above: Talon gets ready for action as Mike draws a bead Right: Two Dartmoor foxes taken with a Sako 85. This is what it's all about!

the intrusion into its world. Sometimes they would just turn and go. Today they would be termed 'lamp-shy' – something I have always had some doubts about. Those early foxes were not lamp-shy as many of them had not been lamped before. I believe there was no 'lamp' involved – they were just shy. Foxes in some ways are not unlike us – they are individuals that vary one from another. Some are bold, fearless and aggressive. Others are shy, wary and a bag of nerves. Then there are the downright curious that are a mixture of the above. They want to find out what the squeak they can hear is, they wonder about the bright light that has suddenly turned night into day, but they are unsure and jumpy. These were, and probably still are, the most vulnerable type.

To get the success we needed, we had to be able to read these foxes soon after they

were spotted. Over time you got to know one or two individuals as their behaviour set them apart from their brethren.

There was, for instance, one dog fox that used to follow us around this cliff land, always keeping out to one side and a little behind us. He would follow us for perhaps half an hour, and even a shot at another fox would not put him off. We tried everything to get him, but to no avail. He would never come in to a call but would drop onto his haunches, sit there like a collie and just watch. If we moved out to him, he would just move away. I suppose today I would wish him luck and let him get on with his life, but years ago we needed to get every fox we could, and this particular animal had been seen paying far too much attention to the lambing flock so we really had to get him.

There was a very large oak tree in the middle of the field in question, and the plan was for one of us to wait there in the dark with the gun while the other would try to 'walk' the fox down the field and eventually get it within range of the waiting gun. I was the walker and Charlie was the hidden gun. Some care would have to be taken as Charlie would be shooting without the aid of a lamp – all illumination would be provided by me. Do bear in mind we were doing this night in and night out, so we had a very good working understanding and safety was paramount.

Arriving at the land, Charlie made his way to the oak, taking a roundabout route while I went to see if I could find the dog fox. Within 10 minutes or so there he was, circling behind me the usual 100 yards or so away. I was about a couple of hundred yards from the oak and hopefully Charlie, so I made the prearranged signal – a couple of quick flashes – to let him know we were on our way.

Even now, after all that time, I can still remember the excitement building as

Calling in the daytime gives far from guaranteed results – but it worked this time

I slowly crossed the field, occasionally flicking the light back to see if the fox was there. Fortunately, he was. Eventually I passed the tree, and when I guessed the fox must have been somewhere within range, I put the lamp full on it and did a hand squeak. As usual, he sat and watched. I could see and hear absolutely nothing, then the sound of the 12 shattered the silence and the fox dropped without a movement.

The plan had worked a treat and we were pleased at the result, but at the same time we felt a little remorse at having ended the life of a fox that we had come to know

quite well. Sentimentality is not really something that people who shoot for a living can allow themselves – the foxes we killed back then provided much-needed money for us, and we were trying to build a reputation as people who could control foxes and prevent stock losses, which could be very high indeed.

That was just one of the many foxes we removed from the area. Most were challenging; a few were easy. The most common way we worked was to spot a fox with the lamp, and once seen, decide on the best way of getting out to it.

Image credit: Tony Hisgett

The light was never shone directly onto it as the approach started. Usually we would flick it on well to one side of where the fox had last been seen. If the eyes were in the same place, we would move extremely slowly and quietly towards it. Occasionally if it showed signs of moving off, we would veer away at right angles but give a few small squeaks to try to hold its interest while giving the impression we were moving away.

Reading the body language of the fox was very important. You got to know when they were on the brink of leaving, and at that moment you needed to let it relax. It is extremely difficult to put into words just how we used to do all of this. It was more a gut feeling and had been learned from countless efforts that had ended in failure. Remember, at this particular time we lived from the proceeds of our shooting efforts. It wasn't sport – we weren't doing it for fun, we needed as many foxes as we could get.

Occasionally even now I will get out a lamp – though definitely not a car headlamp and a 12-volt battery – and stick a gun under my arm and try the old way of shooting a fox. It brings back a host of memories of what was a very free and enjoyable period of my life. Although I remember the way we did it clearly, my skills are rusty and need polishing. Recently I was on some land just having a look round and spotted a fox, probably a vixen some 200 yards away. I had my Benelli 28-bore and a small LED torchlight, and decided to see if I could get out to her using the old methods. Amazingly I got to within about 20 yards of her, and for what seemed an age we watched each other. In the end I told her to clear off, and she did at considerable speed. Where she was she was doing no harm, and for many years now I have followed a policy that I will only

target foxes that are causing trouble – and there are more than enough of them to keep this old man occupied.

The old ways of lamping are behind us. Things, as they always do, move on. We had rudimentary equipment but shot a lot of foxes. It was hard work, long hours, and did not make for a good social or family life. I was out sometimes six nights a week, and although I kept a few records, they have long since disappeared. Numbers of foxes killed weren't tracked scientifically back

then. I would guess that in a good year we got about 400 foxes during the season, and when skins were saleable this would have brought in £5,000-£6,000 – a lot of money in those days. Our efforts were boosted by rabbits and foxes that were wired or shot by others who brought them to me for skinning. We did well, but it was hard work at times.

Time moved on and so did I. After National Service the years flew by and I had a family to support. Eventually I

Above: Lurking in the stubbles as night falls – a good time to be out with the lamp
Above left: Some much-needed practice ahead of a shotgun foxing outing
Left: Out with the Cluson Lazer Light

Big rig: Foxing with a classic Lightforce-style lamp

landed a job with the NFU Mutual, which was probably the best move I ever made. Suddenly I was visiting farmers all over my home county of Devon and was also covering Cornwall. This was in the mid-1960s and it was a very different world from today. As someone linked to the highly respected NFU, I had doors open to me without hesitation. Offers of land to shoot over came almost daily. I always had a gun in the back of the car together with either a spaniel or my fox-killing lurcher Sam, a mighty dog indeed. He was a greyhound/

Irish wolfhound cross. I got him at 18 months old from a girl who was emigrating to Australia and who offered him to me in exchange for a cured fox skin. I said I would try him out first as he had never worked at all. I took him out one night with the lamp, and the first thing this big dog ever killed was a field mouse. That was good enough for me. I took him home and he turned out to be a very good dog indeed. In his time he killed many foxes, rabbits and badgers. That was pre-ban, of course – though one badger would leave him pretty exhausted

as he would pick them up and shake them. Well, he was big.

Word gradually got around that I was good at dealing with foxes, and in those days most lambing was done in the open so foxes presented a real problem. The NFU group secretaries put out a newsletter to their local groups on a monthly basis, and my local chap wrote a small piece about how I had sorted out a fox problem for him in the middle of Torquay of all places. He had a collection of valuable rare breeds of poultry, which he kept in his back garden

in what was then a pretty upmarket area of Torquay, and he had seen at least two foxes taking the birds and was desperate to get rid of them. He got in touch and I went round to look at the area and see what could be done.

The garden was overgrown around the perimeter and had houses on all sides; as far as I could see, a very late night visit when all was quiet was the only solution. A couple of visits at around midnight got no results, but on the third attempt my luck changed. Making my way into the garden

Covering your face and hands pays dividends – and it keeps the midges off

*Power up: Lithium ion
batteries are lighter
and longer-lasting
than the traditional
lead-acid solution*

weapon in the back garden of a house in a respectable area of Torquay. He had been detained by police and would be questioned. How things have changed!

Suddenly I was getting calls coming in from farmers wanting foxes dealt with. It was at this stage I decided to set up a fox control business. I never charged anyone who had a fox problem within my own parish, but for 'outside' work I used to make a small charge, and of course kept the foxes.

One problem that soon became apparent was that a lot of work came in during the early summer when the foxes were active meeting the needs of hungry cubs. Of course the pelts at that time of year were pretty well worthless so the charge had to be raised. I know today many would say they would be more than happy to shoot foxes for nothing in exchange for the right to shoot over the farmer's land. But back when I started the business I had no shortage of shooting rights and I offered a service, pure and simple. If we took no foxes there was no charge. That system works for everyone, it certainly sharpened up our foxing abilities, and to a lesser degree I still offer a fox control service and still get more than enough work.

As time progressed, the lamping equipment we used improved. For a long time we dropped down to a six-volt system using the then new jelly-filled batteries. This was a big step forward as they were so much lighter and didn't wreck your clothes. Lamps, too, gradually improved, and by the 1970s firms like Cluson were producing excellent quality long-lasting lamps – as they do to this day.

Clearly by then there were rumblings by the early anti brigade about the relative merits of selling animal skins. Even then pop stars were making declarations on the rights and wrongs of what went on in the countryside. Gradually the demand for fox

and flicking on the lamp showed two foxes endeavouring to dig under the chickens' run. I was using the lightweight Luigi Franchi five-shot back then, a gun I could shoot one-handed. I brought the gun up; two quick shots had the two foxes dead. A couple of lights went on in the surrounding houses, but apart from that, silence reigned.

Leaving the foxes by the run as proof of success, I went home – at this point it was about two in the morning. The next day I had an early call from the owner of the poultry, who was a happy chap and asked me to go over to his place at midday so he could pay me. Arriving there, I was confronted by a reporter from the local newspaper, who wanted an interview about my fox-shooting exploits. This was duly given, and appeared in the Herald and Express a few days later under the heading "Chicken killers get their just desserts".

I wonder what the reaction would be if the same thing happened today. I suspect the very same paper would be reporting that the police quick response team, backed up by the force helicopter, had apprehended a male suspect armed with an automatic skins and indeed all natural furs declined, culminating in the ban on fur farming in 2000. While I respect people's right to have their own views on all matters, it has always struck me that where foxes are concerned, they are undoubtedly good-looking creatures and their skins, when cured, have a multitude of uses. As it is, because of the actions of certain groups today, just as many foxes are killed but the carcases are dumped as they have no worth. It just seems such a waste.

As it was, things changed, and with the loss of income generated by pelt sales my skinning days were over. I have to say I didn't miss it too much – smelling of fox more or less continuously was something I was happy to leave behind.

The demand for fox control was still there, however, so lamping continued with the continued arrival of better and better lamping equipment. Perhaps it would be appropriate to mention here that I only name those makes of lighting equipment I have personally used – hearsay is pointless in my opinion. There are many other makes of equipment out there; some will be good, some will be bad, so try before you buy.

One of the leading makers of modern lamps is Lightforce, the Australian company that produces car headlamps, founded by Dr Raymond Dennis, who, looking for a lightweight, handheld light for his own use, decided to produce one himself. This was no less than a quarter of a century ago, and today Lightforce still produces some of the best lamping equipment available. Other companies such as Deben, the Suffolk-based company, have also produced an excellent range of lamps, their Tracer brand being particularly good. They also were at the forefront of introducing us shooters to the lithium ion battery. These first appeared about five or six years ago and were incredibly light and long-lasting. Compared

with the old 12-volt lead acid batteries I started with, they were one of the best items to appear on the night shooting scene for years. Today they even have built-in gauges to tell you how much charge is left. Bulbs, too, have changed from the original filament type, with a variety of new types arriving such as halogen, xenon and – coming right up to date – the LED (light-emitting diode).

Top: Late evening foxing on the summer stubbles
Above: The Tracer set-up, a neat package from Deben

A few lamps from the collection. A foxer's kit list can grow at an alarming rate

Modern developments and technology have, as with many things today, allowed items of all sorts to be made more efficient, smaller and lighter. It is getting difficult to call today's lighting equipment 'lamps' – more and more they are becoming 'torches'. Much of the manufacture of these lights is done in China and quality can vary considerably. To myself and I suspect to most other users, one lamp or torch looks very much like another. However, talking to people within the industry has led me to realise that, as with most manufactured products, some are better than others. They may look similar but they can be worlds apart in quality and performance.

Lamps today can have a variety of additional features built in, as can other equipment used at night. Some of the night vision units have quite a lot of accessories and features such as being able to record videos, and watch what is happening on a small screen. Whether these are essential or not is a matter for debate, but they certainly appeal to some and they undoubtedly boost sales.

Lamps today, powered by either halogen or increasingly by LEDs, are extraordinarily powerful. Many are capable of throwing a tight, very white beam out to several hundred metres. I suspect some of the really powerful lamps are a little too powerful

for normal lamping purposes. Certainly I would never use these beams directly on to a fox – lamp-shy or not, few would appreciate that sort of intensity.

What the future of modern lamps holds is open to conjecture, as they seem to me as a mere user to have come as far as they can. I have little doubt, though, that something better will eventually emerge.

There are without a doubt still a considerable number of people who are out and about at night, still using lamps in the traditional way. However, night vision of one sort or another seems to be the modern way. Much lamping is done now from vehicles, with a 'lamper' searching

for fox and a 'shooter' using a rifle. This, I suppose, is about as far away from the old way of setting off on foot as it can be. There is no need for fieldcraft as we knew it – obviously the fox knows you are there. It then comes down to spotting the quarry, judging distance and terrain, and deciding the next step.

The sort of country you are lamping will have the biggest bearing on this. Where I live there are numerous small fields where there are stock, arable and cereal. This is a problem when it comes to foxing from a vehicle, as in most cases gates are shut, preventing rapid access. I have shot at night in various parts of the country, and

Smallbore success: At closer ranges a .22 will do the job

Old and new: The 170 Sport Light, a traditional-style Tracer lamp...

in Hampshire for instance the fields are, to me, vast. If a fox is spotted you can set off in hot pursuit over a considerable distance, but a good shot with a rifle probably doesn't even need to do that. Should the fox turn and move off, you can follow it slowly, and often if not pushed too hard, the fox will more often than not stop and check what's going on. If this is within a couple of hundred yards, there will often

be the chance of a shot. I will confess to not having done a great deal of this type of fox shooting, restricting myself to rabbits when out in a vehicle.

On the subject of rabbits and lamping, the choice of lamp can be quite critical. Many of the modern LED torches that are mounted via a bracket on the scope throw, in my opinion, a far too narrow beam. Rabbits, when lamped from a vehicle,

will, if you drive 30-40 yards out from the hedge, run to the foot of the hedge, where eight times out of ten they will stop. If ever they woke up to the fact that this is a grave error, the numbers of rabbits shot would plummet. Often when at the foot of the hedge they will move about looking for the runs. If the beam is too tight, it is more than easy to lose contact with them.

The best lamp is one that has a good spot and a surrounding 'halo' that covers a decent area. I have for a long time used the Jetbeam BC40, which I have found perfect for the job. Another excellent torch-type lamp is the 4Greer Rangemaster. This, I would suggest, is more of a foxing lamp, as although it has a reasonable halo its biggest asset is its range. On a really dark night the Rangemaster will illuminate out to almost 400 yards, and its battery life is more than enough for several hours lamping.

There is a vast range of this type of gunlight on the market, and like I said, some are far better than others. With any lamp (and, for that matter, with night vision), in most cases you get what you pay

for. Go for one of the better makes and you won't go far wrong.

Personally I am not convinced the torch type is the best for what I would describe as mobile foxing. Though they are ideal for waiting out or when on foot, I find their beams a little too restrictive when riding in a vehicle. For that purpose I return to the more traditional type – either a Lightforce or a Tracer. Equipped with handles, although both can be fitted to a scope, they throw an excellent long-range beam – depending upon the model, as far as 800 metres – while a good spread of light is obtained from the large reflector. Both these makes have a proven track record, and with wiring problems a thing of the past, they represent excellent value for your money. Above all, they do the job.

Lamps have moved on since my young days but the principles involved in lamping the fox remain the same. There are no hard-and-fast rules laid down to guarantee success – as I repeatedly say, foxes vary. Their reactions vary, and what works one night will fail dismally on another. There

...and the 4Greer Rangemaster, a torch-style offering with a near enough 400-yard range

Another lamping excursion ends up with two chicken killers brought to book

are many sources of advice available from magazines, the internet, books and so on, and certainly you will gain some insight into lamping from any of these – but it is how you put it into practice that counts. Again I exclude shooting from vehicles as although it undoubtedly gets results, I feel that the satisfaction gained shooting by this method is nothing compared to pitting your wits against the fox on its own terms at ground level.

The method you will choose depends on how you go about your lamping, and the reasons you have for doing so. As a retired keeper, I know there are times when getting out in the 4x4 with a lamper and a good rifle shot will probably get the best results in terms of numbers. But if you are doing it just to keep the population in check, then lamping on foot is very rewarding and will certainly improve your knowledge both of fieldcraft and the animal you are after.

Despite the massive growth of technology producing such items as night vision and thermal imaging, there will always be the dedicated lamper, many with their more than capable dog, who will rely on the old skills and be out at night 'on the lamp'.

THE FOX

The red fox (*Vulpes vulpes*), the largest of the true foxes, has been with us in this country for centuries, and is widespread throughout the northern hemisphere. It can weigh as little as five pounds and up to about 30 – although in 2012 a dog fox was killed in Scotland weighing in at just over 38lb, and as I write I have recently heard reports of an even larger specimen being shot in England. These are the exception, however – most of the dog foxes I have ever taken the trouble to weigh came out at around 25lb and the vixens around 17lb.

It is not always reliable to sex foxes at a distance by size alone. You will often come across sizeable vixens, and small dog foxes. There can be substantial variations in colour, ranging from very light sandy through all shades to almost black. Very occasionally an albino version appears.

Most foxes remain within a scent-marked territory but others appear to travel at will. These, I suspect, are the ones that give rise to the old saying, "Shoot one fox and two more will appear." If, in their travels, they come across an area with no warning scent markers, they may well move in and remain there.

Family groups remain within their territories, and the subordinate members will often assist in cub rearing. On one area I was keepering, over the boundary was a very pro-hunting farmer, so the foxes were mostly left alone. Clearly some inbreeding had taken place – the main breeding pair and most of the others seen in the vicinity were remarkably alike, all a very pale colour that stood out whenever they were on the move.

The run-up to the actual mating season starts around the end of the year when the calls of both sexes can be heard, particularly on still, frosty nights. The vixen is in season for about three weeks, and after mating, sometimes with a variety of males, gestation lasts about 50 days. Litter sizes vary – they normally range from four to six although up to a dozen have occasionally been observed. Sometimes, however, larger than normal litters can be ascribed to there being more than one family in the same earth. Years ago I saw 13 foxes in a small field at the same time! As far as I could make out, nine were well-grown cubs and four were adults. They were all interacting, and I can only assume they had been brought up together. This can cause confusion when stating the number produced by one vixen. Over my lifetime the biggest litter I knew where all cubs survived to the weaned stage was seven. More often than not though, four or five seems to be the norm. Over the last few years, when rabbit numbers have soared, I have seen numerous litters of five reach early maturity.

After birthing, the vixen rarely leaves the den. This lasts for a couple of weeks at least, as the cubs are unable to regulate their own body temperature. During this time, the dog fox – or sometimes a barren vixen – brings in food. After about five weeks the cubs' eyes change from blue to brown, and the youngsters can be seen leaving the den and playing at the entrance. It is at this stage they begin to eat solid food, brought to them by both parents and sometimes by others of the family group. Lactation itself lasts about six weeks.

Cubs at play: This year's litter is next year's poultry menace

Image: Mark Braggins

As summer wears on, the amount of food brought by the adults tends to tail off, encouraging the cubs to start looking for their own. In the early stages after they are weaned, food consists mainly of mice and voles, but gradually the size of the offerings grows – and it ranges across a very wide spectrum. Rabbits, birds, carrion – practically anything edible will be brought to the hungry growing cubs, including poultry and other things that bring them into conflict with man. (A friend of mine had her husband's suede slippers removed from their living room in London.) By six to seven months the cubs are almost fully grown, and after hunting lessons with the vixen, they start to scatter, although they will remain in the general area for some time to come.

Mortality in the cub population as they start to roam is not uncommon, especially on the roads. One year on the shoot I keepered, I found the carcases of several cubs that had clearly been bitten to death. All I can imagine is that they fell foul of another fox, probably a dog from a neighbouring territory who resented their presence. These had not been eaten – although cannibalism is certainly not unknown among foxes, I doubt cubs would feature as a regular part of the diet.

The earths used for breeding are sometimes old disused badger setts – I have often seen badgers, foxes and rabbits all bringing up families in the same large badger sett. I have to say I don't envy the rabbits in this situation, although for some reason they seem to manage. Other times, foxes will enlarge a rabbit burrow to accommodate the litter. These earths can go back to about six feet with a chamber at the far end. As foxes become more and more accustomed to humans, their breeding sites are more often located around quiet barns, under sheds and so on. The vixen will usually have 'reserve' earths available, and should her cubs be under threat she will move them to a new site. This can be done in a remarkably short time.

Communication among foxes is usually by three methods: vocalising, body posturing and scent marking. At mating time and when the cubs are first on the move, a variety of calls and chattering (gekkering) can often be heard, particularly when the cubs are out hunting with the vixen. The call most people know is the three staccato barks, which can come from both sexes. The scream of the vixen, meanwhile, is the sound most often used by film makers, particularly in horror films. As a lad I was out one early morning in late winter when a thick mist came in. I was quietly moving down the field, tight against the hedge, when a vixen screamed from no more than 15 feet away on the other side of it. The hair stood up on the back of my neck – it really was scary!

All sorts of postures occur when adults meet, varying from enthusiastic, dog-like tail wagging to subservient grovelling by the lower-order members of the community. At mating time or when two male strangers meet, there will often be some quite aggressive behaviour, but this is usually short lived. Mating fights will sometimes end with the loser going off a short distance, hanging around for when the successful male has finished, and then moving in on the vixen.

Finally, scent marking. Dogs and vixens use it for many purposes, but possibly the most important to the fox is territorial marking – although food caches and any obvious markers will all be scent marked within the territory. Scent becomes more obvious to us humans at mating times, when the dog in particular will leave the characteristic musty smell to help attract the vixen and also to keep rivals away. There are several areas that secrete scent, the most pungent being the anal glands. The scent gland on top of the tail near the root spreads scent through the fox lashing and arching its brush. The scent glands under the jaw are used a lot – you will often see foxes rubbing their chins along the ground. Exactly how foxes interpret scent messages is largely unknown to us, but they clearly play a large part in communication between them.

The fox's diet is truly varied. Although it is primarily a carnivore, it will eat almost anything. They commonly consume vegetable matter – I have often seen them feasting on blackberries, and in a friend's garden I have watched foxes standing on their back legs, reaching up to take pears and apples. Mice and voles also are on the menu, and watching a fox mousing can be entertaining, especially if it occurs when snow is on the ground. They eat invertebrates, beetles, and carrion of all sorts from time to time, and of course they are more than happy to raid dustbins. A few years ago I was driving home one night and a fox crossed the road carrying a Kentucky Fried Chicken box in its mouth. As I have said elsewhere, at times foxes and humans are not unalike!

The fox has been hunted throughout the world since, as far as records show, the time of Alexander the Great around 350 BC. Records vary, but some say Edward I had a pack of hounds to hunt the fox with in the 13th century, so what we are doing is nothing new. The way we humans treat foxes has changed throughout history depending on how we view them – at one time they were raised from vermin to 'Beasts of the Chase' by the aristocracy. Even in recent times they were given a degree of protection in hunting country – several keepers of my acquaintance

were asked to leave foxes alone to ensure sufficient numbers for hunting purposes. As an ex-keeper myself, I can imagine the thoughts of those involved!

Whatever views one may have on the fox, one has to admire its ability to survive in a changing world. As we know from the numerous reports and television programmes on the subject, it is firmly established as an urban dweller, and its numbers in that alien environment seem to be increasing year on year.

Back in the late 1950s, as I rode home on my motorbike from the RAF camp in Wiltshire, I often passed late at night through the city of Bath. There was no shortage of foxes roaming the streets – both that city and Bristol had large numbers of foxes inhabiting most areas. The numbers rose substantially until the scourge of mange appeared, and in its inevitable and particularly unpleasant way substantially reduced fox numbers.

I have noticed a similar cycle in the countryside. A farm I have shot over for well over 40 years has a good number of foxes on it because the farmer's wife likes the sight of them, and her husband likes to see them keep the rabbits down – although I have some doubt as to whether this method of rabbit control is efficient! Fox numbers rose in this area until you would see them about by night and day in relatively large numbers. Then mange hit – I suspect it was, in part anyway, because of the artificially high numbers.

Likewise, someone not too far from me who has a strange attitude to wildlife puts out a lot of food for both fox and badger. Again, it was nothing to see up to a dozen foxes hanging around at any one time. Mange was ever-present, and he even obtained a payment from the local residents' association to buy treatment for the foxes when the best method would

have been to stop feeding them in the first place. Still, that's how things change – certainly in my youth I never knew anyone who fed foxes. I hear so many tales of what happens when people interfere with the normal habits of foxes, almost inevitably to someone's detriment.

I live in a rural area that has changed gradually over the years, as many places do, from being populated by people who had lived there all their lives to becoming largely taken over by people from outside. That's all well and good providing they adhere to the way of life in the country, but they don't.

The biggest problem they bring is the persistent feeding of wild creatures. The effect of this is that the foxes and badgers have lost a lot of their natural fear of humans. It is now common to see foxes on a daily basis where not that many years back they would have kept away. This, of course, brings them into contact with poultry, which many of the new country dwellers keep. These luckless fowl almost inevitably get killed by foxes, and then I get called in. If the foxes weren't fed in the first place, the problem would be greatly reduced.

Over the years, despite an increase in the people who shoot them, fox numbers

Above: With the poults comes ever-present fox danger

overall seem to be on the increase. Foxes look alike to most people, and counting them is at best an imprecise science. Accordingly, the figures put out by various organisations differ, but they always seem to end up around the 250,000 mark or higher. These figures are arrived at in the main by faecal counts; personally I think fox numbers are substantially higher than this. I can only speak from knowledge of the area over which I shoot and until recently keepered. But there is little doubt in my mind that over the last 10-15 years numbers have risen. Some of this is down to artificial feeding, and substantial rabbit numbers at the foxes' breeding time. Also

in the past couple of years I have owned a thermal imager, a Pulsar Quantum HD38. This has totally changed my thoughts on just how many foxes are out there. With the thermal imager you see everything out to 500 yards or even more, and it's true to say I have been amazed as to just how many there are.

As the fox goes about its business, much of which is the search for food, certain aspects of its behaviour will inevitably bring it into conflict with humans. I am referring to foxes that live in the countryside, as the urban fox is almost a different creature. When I first started controlling foxes it was done purely to make money from their skins, so during the suitable time of year, usually from October to March, I would take every fox I could by whatever means were available. I was young and needed the income, and every fox represented much-needed cash. I gradually became known in the area, so quite a lot of farmers came to me asking for help in getting rid of the foxes. In those days, as far as I can remember, there were few who did what I did – it was years before I actually met another fox controller.

I exclude keepers from that as their approach was a little different. There were three keepers locally, all of whom I knew well. All of them were happy for me to deal with their foxes as they had heavy workloads. Keepers do today as well, of course, but back then a lot of the birds were reared under broody hens, and believe me, the work involved was tremendous, giving the keeper precious little time to wander about looking for foxes.

I began to learn that there were certain times of year when foxes were a greater nuisance than usual. These are obvious when you look at it. Lambing time, game bird rearing time, and of course when cubs are being raised. In those days winter was, in reality, the only time I was interested in catching foxes, as during the summertime skins were useless. But where help was asked for, I did the job and on rare occasions got paid something for my trouble. This, I suppose, sowed the seed for what I was to do much later on in my life.

My view of foxes has changed considerably over the years. In the first flush of youth I killed without much thought, and never gave a great deal of thought to the consequences as far as the fox itself was concerned.

As years passed I learned much more about the creature I sought to kill and the way it lived its life, and I grew to respect it. Clearly the things foxes do that cause

strife with us humans are done not from vindictiveness or malice, but from a need to survive. Whatever you may think, you can hardly blame a fox for taking a free-ranging hen wandering about the field unprotected, can you? To the fox it is just an easy meal. I keep chickens and have, much to the amusement of some of the village, lost hens to foxes and badgers. With one exception it was my own fault, in the same way most call-outs I get to deal with problem foxes are brought about by the human, not the animal.

Foxes are omnivores. They will eat virtually anything, and I have the feeling that, like most predators, they rather 'enjoy' killing. I don't mean in the way a human serial killer enjoys killing – as humans, they are supposed to have a reasoning facility in their brain, so they derive stimulation and pleasure from what they do. Nor is it exactly like the domestic cat, a ruthless predator. As far as I can see, it kills purely and simply from instinct, and derives apparent pleasure from catching, tormenting and finally killing its hapless victim. All that on a stomach full of Whiskas, so it has no need to kill. The fox, on the other hand, isn't killing essentially for pleasure but for survival. Where the problem arises is where they go 'over the top'.

How many times have I heard someone who has just had a visit from a fox say, "I wouldn't have minded if it had just taken one"? They usually follow this by wondering why foxes go on killing sprees. Many have given their views on the subject, but what is clear is that foxes do not have the capacity to reason in the same way as we do. A fox is wired to kill. Its reactions are unbelievably quick, and the senses that trigger them are something we can only wonder at. I have watched foxes on the hunt come across a rabbit unexpectedly, and in an instant they have it. Most of their

true hunting, as opposed to scavenging, runs on reflex. Deep down they expect the prey to try to get away, so they act as swiftly as they can. The vast number of hunts the fox makes throughout its life are over extremely quickly: there is one target, a quick strike, then success or failure.

Suddenly the scene changes – this conditioned super-killer finds a chicken run. It doesn't know it's a chicken run – all it sees and smells is food. It finds its way in and strikes. The hunt should be over, but suddenly there is another flapping, clucking hen, not flying away but running past within striking distance. The fox reacts to its deep-seated instincts and strikes again, and again until there are no more flapping, panicking hens. It has reacted to its programming.

Many years ago I was called out to a farm where lambs were being taken. Shortly after I spotted a fox approaching the flock. Bolder than most I had seen, it wasn't phased by stamping ewes, and made its way into the centre of the bunched-up sheep. Newborn lambs were everywhere and it wasn't long before the fox was sniffing at still-wet navel cords and nibbling at afterbirth. I watched as it got into a state of excitement and started nipping at lambs' ears and tails. I got the impression that its thoughts were, 'It's here – let's get on with it.' A shot eventually presented itself, and it was over. This was in the lamping days, by the way, and I watched this entire scene unfold by the illumination of the lamp.

How many shooters in their time have killed far more pigeons, rabbits and other quarry than they have had use for? I have done just this in the past. We can perhaps justify it by virtue of crop protection, population control and so on, but in the first instance it could have simply been that they were there. To the fox in the chicken run or release pen, it's much the

same: they were there, so let's have a go. So often they try to catch prey that just runs or flies away, so when they find themselves in an artificial situation where the prey cannot escape, they will kill and kill.

Foxes, of course, will cache food and come back to it; we, of course, will put a few pigeons in the freezer. Sometimes I think we are not that different from the fox!

The onus is upon the keepers of livestock to ensure their charges are protected. So many times have I heard, "I don't like shutting my hens in – I love seeing them out in the field," and I do understand the reasoning behind this. But there is every chance the fox will call. They are very persistent hunters. Again, so often someone people say, "That was just bad luck. I shut my birds in every night, but this once I forgot, and the fox got in." What they need to realise is that the fox is there night after night doing the rounds. I use trail cameras quite a lot I see the same foxes every night. In this respect they are not like us. If we go to a shop three or four times and it is always

shut, we go somewhere else. Foxes, on the other hand, will patrol their territory every night, and every so often they get lucky.

There is only one way to keep your poultry safe, and that is to shut it into fox-proof houses and runs at all times. But sometimes even this doesn't work. I am pretty careful with my hens, and they are in the adjoining field in full sight of the house. The large run is protected the same way I used to protect the pheasants: normal fencing with a double strand of wire connected up to a 12-volt energiser. One night a badger ripped through the fence, totally ignoring the inevitable electric shock, and managed to get the pop hole sliding door up and get inside the coop. Unfortunately for the badger, the pop hole slid down again, trapping it inside. It slaughtered all but one of the birds in there before I could get there and sort things out.

Foxes don't possess the strength of the badger, but they certainly have persistence and will spend a considerable length of time seeking a weak spot in a fence or coop.

The badger: A divisive figure in the countryside today

Lambs: One of the fox's favourites

The fox is the supreme opportunist, and seldom misses a chance to grab a meal. It behoves us to look after our poultry and protect it, but sometimes, as many keepers will tell you, no matter how careful you are the fox will succeed.

The fox's predatory habits will always bring it into conflict with humankind, but sometimes I wonder whether there are times it is blamed for crimes it was not wholly responsible for. In the lambing field, for example, it is constantly held responsible for the killing of lambs, and there is no doubt that it does just that. But I suspect that, though it may take the odd healthy specimen, quite a lot of its spoils are leftovers such as skins and legs that belonged to lambs that were already dead or at least well on the way out. Foxes are above all scavengers, so an all-but-dead lamb would be easy pickings.

Having watched them on many occasions preparing to take a lamb, I have noticed that they are very nervous killers. They will often just scavenge afterbirths, or warily wander around the flock looking for isolated singles or doubles, although I have a feeling they have a preference for the latter. A single stamp from the ewe, should she be in attendance, will have the fox veering off.

Eventually, should the predator chance upon a single or double where the ewe is grazing away, it will get bolder and close in. After circling a few times, it will gingerly reach out, usually at full stretch, and very gently take a grip on the fleece. These early-born lambs do absolutely nothing to resist, and very slowly the fox tugs at the lamb, getting it away from its sibling. When it is five or six yards away it seems to get excited and will then start to nip at either their ears, the navel or the tail.

It is at this juncture, whenever I have watched this, that the potential killer turns into the victim as I shoot it. I assume that the next stage of the event would have been a bite to the neck. On small game such as rabbits and fowl, all that is needed is a bite to the neck, or often in the case of birds, across the back.

Killers they most certainly are, and they can be ruthless in the extreme, but as in most of their lives, foxes are wary, nervous creatures when hunting. It is this wariness that much of the time keeps them safe.

I once had a pet fox that I caught as a very small cub. I reared it at home where, at the same time, I had two terriers and a lurcher, all working on fox! I successfully reared it to adulthood but it really was like a game of chess, especially when moving the fox, as all doors would have to be shut and the terriers' whereabouts known.

In the end it all got too much and I gave the fox, which was very tame, to, of all people, a keeper friend of mine. He had it for nearly five years before, I believe, it was shot. It was an interesting experience and I learned a lot from the cub – it was very tame and playful, but a bit destructive. After it had left me I learned that it ran with the keeper's dogs, and was treated just like one. It would go off at mating times but would always return to be fed. Do they make good pets? No. Would I do it again? No. But it was an experience I wouldn't have missed.

The fox is an enterprising and intelligent creature that has survived all we can throw at it. Even today, with advanced technology and wondrous gadgets that allow us to enter its world more than ever, it still thrives. For that, be it friend or foe, hats off to the fox.

THE USUAL METHODS OF CONTROL

Shooting may be the most used method of fox control today, but there are other ways to get on terms with this wily predator. What I want to do in the coming chapters is pass on some fox control tips, particularly those for newcomers, and dispel some of the myths that have grown up around the fox over the years. Before starting, let me say I am aware that there are many people out there who shoot large numbers of foxes today, and they undoubtedly could teach me a thing or two. All I can claim is that I have been after the fox for over 60 years, so I must have learned something.

The first thing to remember is that foxes never do anything invariably. Just when you think you have them sussed, they prove you wrong yet again. Calling them is a prime example. There are a multitude of calls and callers on the market, all 'guaranteed' to get foxes flying in to you as fast as they can – but it just doesn't happen like that. All calls will work to a degree, some better than others, but do we ever try to work out why? The answer to that has to be no. It's probably an impossible question anyway as we really don't know what triggers a fox to respond. Hunger has to be the prime factor, as a hungry fox will without doubt respond to a call far better than one that has a belly full of food. However, a full fox will still show interest

at times – down, I suspect, to curiosity more than anything else. Don't forget that they are programmed to kill, so if they hear a distress call they may well investigate.

The reason few of us learn much about our chosen quarry is that we usually shoot it. You will learn little from a dead fox but a great deal from a living one. As I have got older I have spent an increasing amount of time observing the creature I have pursued for so many years. As a result, I have begun to doubt a few things I was told years ago by those who have now long gone. Not all – just a few.

I am fortunate to live in an area where there is a high population of truly wild foxes. I have lived here for a long time, and have virtually free rein over the whole area to go where I want by night and day. I have learned where the foxes are, where they breed and where they go when they are out and about. The more I watch, the more I learn.

For example, calling foxes by day and night has always fascinated me. It is one aspect of fox control that can be immensely exciting and rewarding, and at times totally frustrating. Why should a fox that will run in to a call one night totally ignore it the next? The problem we humans have is trying to work out what a fox hears. Certainly it hears the same sounds as we

At home in the garden. Any fox visiting Mike's hens in summer will only be doing it once!

do, but its highly developed senses must also hear much more. Some say it can hear a mouse squeak 100 yards away. Only a fox could say if this is true, but what is certain is that they certainly know the real thing from our efforts to replicate it.

I have used a variety of calls, from the excellent WAM caller (much like my Hornby railway carriage wheel from bygone years) to modern digital devices such as the FoxPro range, and at some point with each of them, I have experienced the same event. It has happened in a variety of situations – waiting in concealment during a summer evening, or lurking under the cloak of darkness. My calls are doing well at times, failing dismally at others, as I try to pull a fox in to take a closer look. Suddenly, within range of my own hearing, another fox or a stoat catches a live rabbit, which screams. Instantly the fox that has been thinking about checking out my call is gone. There was no hesitation – it knows that call is genuine. So all I can learn from this is that our calls are more objects of curiosity than anything else. We have all had foxes come in at a gallop – usually, these are cubs out hunting on their own for the first time, or old foxes that have been fooled or are extremely hungry, and are prepared to throw caution to the winds.

Then there are people like Pat Carey (the Warrener), who I have the greatest respect for as he has perfected the art of calling the fox better than pretty well anyone else, mainly using the traditional method of squeaking, either by mouth alone or with the mouth-hand combination. It can be done, but as more and more people try their hand (or FoxPro) at calling the fox, perhaps we are in danger of making him more suspicious. Certainly, 60 or so years ago foxes were not being called as much as they are today, and the success rate I had was more or less the same as it is now, despite

the host of calls that has become available since then.

So how do I go about calling them in? During daylight, particularly in late summer when cubs are out hunting, I try any spot near cover, particularly if foxes have been seen in the vicinity. My advice is to just tuck yourself away and have a call. Cubs are not that savvy and will turn up from almost any direction at a gallop. You may need to give them a shout or a whistle as they come in to stop them for a moment, as they will often just keep coming – fine with a shotgun but not with a rifle.

I have not found wind direction to matter too much during the day – foxes these days are seldom far from humans, and are used to their scent. At night, it really pays to have done some research and know roughly where your foxes are. I'm talking about walking, not driving round.

If I think (or know) there has been a fox or two about, I will get there about an hour before dark, and pick a decent spot to wait. This will be, if possible, somewhere with a good field of view, and preferably where I know foxes have been travelling. Then I will settle down to wait. Using a thermal

Above: A good spot for a digital fox caller. Foxes will often stand underneath it
Left: Calling the old-fashioned way, and possibly still the best

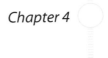

Top left: The Foxpro Spitfire can be deadly when used at the right time
Top right: The Faulhaber is ideal for close calling
Above: Typical run through a hedge

imager or night vision will certainly give you an advantage if you can afford it. Scanning with the thermal will pick up a fox anywhere out to 400 yards, sometimes more. After that, use a fairly strident call like the Best Fox Call (Tenterfield type) to attract a fox's attention, and with luck it will come in your direction.

Opinions differ as to whether you change the call the closer the fox gets. Some advocate changing to a mouse squeak. Personally I'm not too sure about this – after all, the fox was attracted to the rabbit call in the first place,

and will surely be confused if the screaming rabbit suddenly changes to a squeaking mouse! But if it comes in so far, then stops, a change of tactics may work. Generally I try to drop the volume of the call I am using, as often when a fox or other predator is making a kill, the cries of the victim become less strident as the end approaches. In my experience, though, you can seldom lay down hard-and-fast rules – foxes, like people, all have a different take on things.

If you spot a fox while driving round your land, more often than not in this day and age you will have a good chance of a shot with a rifle. There will also be times, though, when a fox will make off. At these times, it is a quick call, shout or whistle that may attract its attention long enough for the shot to be taken.

One of the best times to do some calling is during the late summer months, a couple of hours before dark. Both adult and cubs nearing maturity will be on the move, as it will have been many hours since their last meal. A small point here: foxes, like most things, are ruled by the need to feed themselves and, at certain times, their families. Concerning the latter, the parents as the cubs grow will be desperate for food, and it's then they are at their most

troublesome. Under normal conditions, during the non-breeding season they will be far more likely to hunt when the prey species are about, mainly at the onset of darkness. It is then they are most vulnerable and likely to respond to calling.

Unless you are into remote digital callers, you will use either one of the many proprietary calls or your hand – in terms of this selection, my advice is to use the calls you are familiar with. Be warned, though – foxes have the ability to pinpoint exactly where the sound is coming from, and this can present problems. For example, I was set up in the corner of a field in waist-high nettles looking down the line of the hedge where I knew a fox was travelling. It had been taking poultry and had to go. The trouble is that when you start to call you often have no idea where the fox may be, and although they follow their runs, they do stray from these on a regular basis.

In this instance, as the fox hadn't shown after an hour or so, I decided on a call. Why hadn't I called before? Because if you are shooting foxes selectively and are after one particular individual, if you call you stand a good chance of bringing in the wrong animal. I decided to give the WAM a try followed by the Faulhaber Hazel Grouse Hen call – a very good call for close work.

Within minutes I heard a noise in the hedge next to me. Something, obviously a fox, was in the nettles about five yards in front of me. I watched its progress by the waving nettle heads but couldn't see the fox. Eventually as it was so close it got wind of me and was gone. A few minutes later exactly the same thing happened again, and then again. Three foxes had come to the call but because of bad positioning I didn't get a shot in at any of them. As some sort of excuse I have to say I was in the only part of the field where a safe shot could be taken

Using the Faulhaber call as a fox comes in to a closer distance

*Tweed and moleskins
– still as effective a
form of camo as any*

anyway. Bad reconnaissance let me down – my own fault, and really I should have known better.

When calling, particularly in daylight finding the best place is vital – you never know from where the fox will appear. Say you have hillside with clumps of bramble scattered over it, which looks like good fox country. My advice is not to go onto that hillside and call – almost certainly, the fox will be upon you before you know it. Better to find a spot where you can look into the hillside. Although it may mean shooting at longer ranges, the results should justify it. Location is vital, but how you conceal yourself is an equal crucial matter, whether you are foxing by day or by night. The obvious place is tucked away in a hedge, but there you are at ground level, which can pose problems both from safety and visibility perspectives. Then there is the portable high seat. Provided you have somewhere to set it up, this is ideal – safe and with excellent visibility. Finally, your pick-up, car or 4x4. Don't discount vehicles – most foxes see them on a daily basis, and will often totally ignore them as long as you keep still enough. I now use my 4x4 as a shooting 'hide' more often than not, and as far as I am aware it hasn't stopped foxes from going about their normal business. The more I see of the modern fox, the more

I realise it just accepts vehicles as part and parcel of normal life.

Finally, a tale of just how unpredictable foxes' reactions to calls can be. A friend of mine in the village was decorating his kitchen early in the year, and even though it was really cold he had the window open as the smell of paint in the small room was a bit overpowering. The woodburner was churning out a good heat and a bit of smoke – enough, in fact, to trigger the smoke alarm. Within a few moments a fox, which had clearly heard the alarm's typical 'wheep, wheep' came running down the field that backed on to the cottage and arrived right under the open window. Perhaps a smoke alarm, a piece of oily rag and a box of matches should be in every fox shooter's pocket!

There are scores of calls out there, and it really is a matter of trying them out to find which one works for you. Although digital callers reproduce actual sounds, after they have been through the speaker system I am not sure if the fox hears them in the same way we do. If they did, surely they would come running in every time you played it. Of course, they don't.

I have been calling foxes all my life, and the only thing that's certain about is that you can never guarantee results. Remember, foxes do not all do the same things invariably.

I mentioned night vision earlier – this really can help you get results. I have found that using a thermal imager and night vision in conjunction gives you a big advantage, especially if you are after a particular fox. This combination is, at the time of writing, possibly the best set-up you can get. Spotting first with the thermal, you will see every living creature within your field of vision.

Should you spot a fox, then depending on its behaviour you will have to pick your

next move. If you recognise it as the fox you are after, then in reality you should be in a position you would expect the animal to arrive at without the need for calling. The best example of this is where poultry has been taken. You would probably have set up in a spot where you have a good view of the surrounding area, a line of sight to where poultry was taken, and above all, a safe direction to shoot. It is pointless getting into a position and waiting for hours only to be forced to let the quarry go because a safe shot couldn't be taken. You can't stop this happening occasionally, but unless you are just heading out in the vague hope of nailing any old fox, forward planning will tip the scales in your direction. If all these criteria have been observed, it should only be a matter of time before the fox comes within range of its own accord.

In my opinion, if you have gone to the considerable expense of getting good quality night vision, then lights are definitely off limits, except of course to go and collect your fox when you have shot it. To this end, unless I am certain of getting the fox, I let it go on its way and try again later. If you have not disturbed it, then in all probability it will turn up later for another look round.

Of course foxes are unpredictable, and the fox you are after may not immediately arrive exactly where you want it. But the way I would deal with it, again, is to stay put and wait. I might possibly try a call, but too much calling can put foxes off. Just think of how often you hear animal distress cries when out at night. I hear the odd rabbit squeal and a very few other sounds, but certainly not incessant calls, and sometimes I think calling can be overdone.

One thing I have not mentioned is patience and the ability to keep still for long periods. Movement is what most creatures, us included, see first. A good deerstalker will move a few steps then freeze and see what is moving – often even the flick of a roe's ear will give the game away, something you wouldn't have spotted when on the move. If you watch a fox hunting, they constantly stop and survey the area. They do this for the same reason the experienced stalker does: to see movement and hear sounds.

Foxes have a reputation for intelligence, but I suspect much of their lives is governed by instincts that have been embedded in their brains and bodies over centuries. We can only imagine what these instincts tell them. Ours, no matter how good we think we are, have been dulled over the same centuries, and most of us are clumsy blunderers compared with the fox, particularly at night. In my case I prefer to think carefully about how I am going to deal with a particular fox, have a good look at the land, and make a plan, which usually consists of picking my best area, getting there and waiting. More often than not if you have the patience, the fox will arrive. This may not happen the first night or even the second, but unless it has been seriously disturbed or killed elsewhere, it will turn up eventually.

I would stress that this is the way I go about fox control today using the technology that is available to me. In the past I used to walk the fields endlessly at night and shoot a lot of foxes, but it was utterly random. Today virtually all the foxes I shoot are those that have caused or will cause problems. I have to be as certain as I can that I have got the right one.

On another matter, something I and many others in the countryside do when after foxes is keep an eye on the other creatures that are out and about. Few animals or birds are happy in the company of the fox, and using their reactions will often tip you off when Charlie is about.

Probably the best known is the rabbit, who above all others has reason to be wary of the fox. At night or at any other time when rabbits are out, they will soon let you know a fox is on the move. The three main indicators are a mad rush to the hedge (fox getting uncomfortably close), rabbits sitting bolt upright and staring fixedly in one direction (he's over there somewhere), and finally the bush-telegraph system of bumping, caused by the rabbits stamping hard, usually a couple of times with their back feet. This will spread at great speed down hedges, and is usually the forerunner of the sitting up posture.

I am sure many who use night vision will have seen the opposite behaviour where rabbits seemingly ignore a fox crossing a field at night. I think this is usually because of one of two things: either the fox is not in hunting mode, or because the rabbits have a clear view of their sworn enemy and are ready for flight if necessary.

During daylight crows and magpies will mob a fox. If it is in the open, they will dive-bomb the animal, passing on occasions within inches of it. I have got many a fox in the past by watching crow activity and getting ahead of the moving fox. Often they will be distracted by the corvids and become less wary.

Songbirds too will give out warning sounds when a fox is about. Top of the list has to be the blackbird – the gentle but insistent pip, pip, pip will give you a good idea of where the predator is moving. Blackbirds will follow a fox through woodland or down hedgerows, and particularly in the evening this will pinpoint his position rather well. A word of warning, though: the alarm sound of the blackbird is almost identical for fox and cat. There is a minute difference, but you can only tell when you are familiar with both calls.

Other small birds like robins and great tits will often give out warning sounds, particularly at nesting time. The reaction of these various animals to foxes is interesting – it must be bred into them. In truth I can't see foxes being a major threat to, say, a blue tit, but these little birds really don't like them!

I mentioned elsewhere the reaction of some cattle to foxes. The same applies to most stock. Horses will often gaze fixedly at a spot where a fox may be lying or working. The sounds of a flock of lambing ewes will be very different if a fox is hanging about the flock. There will be restlessness and much calling of ewe to lamb – very different to the relaxed atmosphere when the fox is elsewhere.

Keepers will be aware that pheasants sometimes warn of a fox's approach, although on other occasions they seem unaware of the danger they may be in. Many years ago there was a shoot in my village, and there are still some descendents of those birds around. They can probably be described as 'wild' now. These birds are certainly far more wary than the ones I used to put to wood. Perhaps because of the pheasant's somewhat dubious reactions to vermin, many keepers will put a couple of guinea fowl in the pens with the pheasants. These strange birds will certainly let you

The poults can be a good early warning system of a fox's presence, but better still are the guinea fowl or blackbird

know if there is a fox about – the only downside of this is that they will shout at practically everything else as well. And they do rather let everyone know where the pen is – not always a good thing.

In short, when you are out and about in the country after the fox, keep an eye on what else is going on around you. The reactions of other creatures will often let you know where your quarry is.

Weather can play a big part in getting you a fox. Over the years I have discovered that foxes' likes and dislikes where weather is concerned are similar to our own. Clearly they have to get their food, but in wet and windy conditions in particular, they are inclined to keep their heads down. Equally they like a bit of sun on their backs – you can pick up the odd one enjoying a sunbathe! If you live in a hilly area, a quiet walk round on a winter's day when the sun has decided to put in an appearance will often find a fox laid up in a sheltered spot on the side of a hill where it will get the full benefit of the sun. Use the stalker's techniques of progressing slowly with frequent stops to scan the hillside with your binoculars. If you take it steadily and don't rush, you will often come across a fox sound asleep.

Stalking foxes can bring rewards but extreme care needs to be taken. I would place silence as the most important factor, certainly well ahead of scent. In many areas today, foxes live side by side with humans, and our scent is just part of their everyday life, but their extraordinarily hearing abilities will soon pick up alien sounds. If they do, they will be off in a flash. Incidentally, while on the subject of the fox's hearing ability, the one sound guaranteed to spook them and most other wild animals is metal. This is totally alien to wild animals, so if you are stalking them, make sure your safety catch is silent – even

the click of its operation can be enough to get them on the move.

Many animals adapt to circumstances, and the fox is no exception. There is a wildlife park where I occasionally need to reduce the fox population, as not only do they carry the danger of mange but they have also been known to take the young of some of the resident animals. The interesting thing here is that during the day when visitors are about, foxes can be seen lying out in the sun in some of the paddocks, or going about their business, totally ignoring the many people that at times come feet of them. When I first went there it was during the day, and I remember thinking it was going to be really easy money – all I would have to do was walk round after the park closed, and shoot a few foxes with the .22 as they sat and watched me.

I couldn't have been more wrong. As soon as the park was empty of visitors and staff, the foxes became incredibly wary – if anything they were even warier than their country brethren. At the first sign of me they would be gone like a flash. Fortunately the park had various viewing points that served well as high seats, and as is often the case, patience won the day. My routine was to get to the park as the last visitors left, and then while the staff were finishing up for the day, get into position. Almost as soon as the last staff member left, the foxes would appear, and each night one or two would drop to the .22LR. By not overdoing it and only going there once every two weeks or so, I could reduce the fox numbers to acceptable levels.

Foxes are quick to notice changes in their environment – even around habitation, it is best to leave things exactly as they normally are. When I am waiting around a house where perhaps a fox has had the chickens, the residents often say to me, "We will keep the lights off and not make any noise." More often than not this is the

worst thing you can do. Keep things normal – if lights are usually on, leave them on. If curtains are never drawn, don't draw them. Foxes are not stupid – they notice changes in their surroundings and this will always make them suspicious.

Finally, you have done all the work, you are in the right place and the fox has appeared on cue. The time has come for the shot – this may well be the one chance you get, after hours of waiting in the cold and the wet. Your reputation as a fox controller has come down to this moment in time. The last thing you want to do is miss.

It happens to all of us. I have missed sitters in my time and will undoubtedly do it again, but all you can do is lessen the chances of missing that elusive fox as much as possible. What I try to do is to wait for the moment when the perfect target is presented. This probably applies to the use of night vision more than conventional lamping – often with the latter you have to be quick or the chance may be gone. At times it may be better to let the animal go and try again next time, as a shot at fox will be reluctant to return. In most cases when using night vision you will have more time than you think to take the shot, so wait for it to pause in its wanderings. Should it show signs of moving off, a small noise will more often than not get its attention long enough for you to get the job done.

I often think of a particular person who once phoned me up to tell me he was a fox shooter, had shot more than 1,000 foxes and never missed one. I was truly humbled and could only wish that perhaps even now at my age I, with practice, could become as good as he was!

In high summer, a troublemaker taken in a tramline through the rape crop

ALTERNATIVE METHODS

I have discussed using night vision and lamps when after foxes at night, but there are other ways to get on terms with the predator. Daylight shooting is not often discussed at any length, but it can be successful if you know a bit about your quarry. I have said before that unfortunately when people start out shooting foxes, their sole desire is to do just that – shoot them. Apart from getting an idea of how old it is (teeth and condition) and what it has been feeding on (stomach contents), you learn precious little from a dead fox. When watching a fox come in to your call or to a bait point you learn a little, but if you wait a little longer, you could learn a whole lot more.

When I was young, and when I was keepering, I never waited to see what a fox was up to. I just wanted results. I dispatched foxes as quickly and as humanely as possible. In my later years I have changed, not only in some of the ways I go about dealing with foxes but also in my attitudes. Most of the foxes I deal with today are causing problems, usually taking lambs or poultry. These have to be dealt with – you cannot expect people to put up with having valuable livestock taken. However, I no longer shoot foxes on sight – I now feel that if they are in a situation where they are doing no harm, they should be left alone. I have been told that this is just a way of ensuring a good supply of foxes for me to shoot in the future, and I would be the first to agree that virtually every

fox is a potential killer and sooner or later will come into conflict with us humans. So perhaps that point of view is not far wrong! But I have found that when you don't shoot every fox on sight, you learn more about the animal.

By watching I have learned that there are certain times when the fox is active during daylight hours. Early in the morning – I should say here that I am talking about the late spring/summer months, not the depths of winter – foxes can be seen returning to their earths or lie-ups after a night's hunting.

Some say foxes are good timekeepers, but I am not so sure. So often I had heard that such-and-such a fox will always be seen at around 7.30am, but although foxes will travel their territory fairly regularly, timekeeping is not top of their agenda. Foxes do not go out for a walk – they go to hunt, and if successful the either make their way back from whence they came or lie up for a sleep. So depending on the type of land you are shooting over, a bit of reconnaissance is seldom a waste of time.

If you select a high vantage point and tuck yourself away with a pair of binoculars, you could well be surprised at what you will see. No shooting – just wait, watch and learn. A couple of outings like this will tell you far more than just tramping round your land in the hope of seeing something. Using this method, the fox will often know you are there long before you are aware of him, and will slip away. All this observation

might boring but it has always served me well, and once you know where the foxes are running, cubbing and hunting, you can deal with the matter as you see fit.

I do exactly the same at night using a thermal imager. Since these remarkable items have become available I have discovered how little I actually knew about the number of foxes that run over the land around me. Spotting foxes at night out to 500 yards or so, though it obviously doesn't offer a shot, will give you a good indication of where they are and the routes they are taking.

Returning to the daylight hours, between midday and about 2pm is a good time to wait out for foxes during the summer months. I said before that I am not an advocate of shooting vixens when they have cubs just for the sake of it. That's true,

Image credit: Mark Braggins

but there have been times when as a keeper and fox controller I have done it without a second thought. In those situations, those vixens were regular poultry killers and had to be dealt with – if the opportunity came up in the daytime, it couldn't be wasted.

This is where observation comes into play again. Whenever I took out a troublesome vixen during the breeding season I always tried to know where the cubs were located. Then when the vixen was dealt with, it was generally an easy matter to mop up the cubs. For the sake of spending a few hours watching where the adults were coming and going, I could more or less pinpoint where the earth was and with it the cubs.

Incidentally, it does not automatically follow that when the vixen is killed the cubs will starve. Clearly if this happens in the early days when they are living on her milk, they will succumb, and pretty quickly too. But after they are weaned it is a different matter altogether. Not only will the dog fox bring food back to them, but within the family group there will be other relatives that will fill the gap left by the vixen.

Some years ago I knew of an earth where there were four newly weaned cubs. The vixen was a tatty little thing with some mange about her. I had been watching this family with interest as they were across a steep valley and the farmer to whom the land belonged to was a big hunting man, so the foxes were left alone.

One morning I was driving up the valley road and came across the vixen dead where she had been hit by a car. That evening I was in my usual vantage point across the valley, 200 yards as the crow flies from the earth. I was intrigued to see what would happen, as by then the vixen would have been absent for 12 hours or more. The first adult fox that showed was the dog, a big, rangy animal with noticeable whitish patches on

his flanks. He carried a rabbit with him into the earth. Over the next couple of hours two more foxes visited the earth, one carrying a magpie. One of these, presumably a barren vixen, had similar whitish markings to the dog, so I assumed it was a family member, possibly one of last year's cubs.

This litter reached maturity, and probably ended up being shot by me as they spread out onto my shoot! The point I am trying to make here is that I would never have found out any of this if the foxes were just shot on sight. Observation can advance your knowledge far more than you might think.

Calling foxes by daylight can also work well. In my experience, cubs out hunting for the first few times are pretty gullible, and will often be out and about during the day honing their new found skills. Small rodent calls work well on them, as much of their early training from the old foxes will have entailed killing this type of prey: short-tailed field voles, field mice and young rabbits. Imitating their calls will work well on hunting cubs.

After 2pm, I have found things go a bit dead where foxes are concerned. In fact, few of our native mammals do much after this time until the late evening. About an hour before full dark is when foxes start to think about moving out. Much depends on location – if you have a really quiet area during the late summer, you could come across cubs out on the hunt at almost any time, with the old foxes just lying out in the late evening sun. I live in a hilly area; here the foxes seek out the west-facing

Above: Younger foxes are especially vulnerable to the daytime foxer
Left: Daylight foxing works well on this occasion

*Top: Tilling a wire
Above: Wires set
around the pen can
catch well. This one
is set too low*

a more leisurely approach – watching, waiting and observing – will pay dividends in the long term, not only in the numbers you shoot but also in the accumulation of knowledge that will serve you well over years to come.

Another method of dealing with troublesome foxes is trapping. Snares (or wires) have been used to catch animals for centuries using a variety of methods. Many of these methods are illegal in this country – indeed, political legislation is starting to take more than a passing interest in snaring today. Scotland is at the forefront of moves to make snaring more acceptable, and those involved in trapping have to register and tag their traps.

Snaring foxes is effective when done correctly – and some people are very good at it indeed. My farmer friend from 50 or so years ago Gordon was a master at it. He would, seemingly without any effort, catch fox after fox. Another I knew from my youth was old Bill Martin. His interest lay with rabbits, not foxes, and as boys Johnny and I would watch old Bill walk across the hillside putting down wire after wire almost without breaking step – just bend, stamp the short peg in, stick in the tealer, move the wire slightly and move on. He would lay scores in this way in the space of half an hour or so.

Although I have caught many rabbits and foxes in wires, I could never be classed as an expert in the ranks of those two. Gordon would try to explain how he did it, but the thing you can never really impart to those who wish to learn is the 'feel' for what you are doing. This comes only with years of experience, trial and improvement. I sometimes wonder at the way things are today, when aspiring shooters – particularly where deer are concerned – take a couple of courses and become (in their mind at least) experts. Courses are

hillsides to catch the last of the day's sun. Once again, tucking yourself away with a decent pair of binoculars will often reveal the odd fox curled up, enjoying the last of the warmth.

Perhaps I come from a different time, when we went about things a bit more carefully. From what I see and hear, many people these days taking up fox shooting start off at a gallop. I have found that often great in setting out the welter of legislation that now exists, again particularly where deer are concerned, but they can never teach a 'feel' for the land and the creatures that inhabit it. Increasingly legislation will force more and more obligatory courses for those wishing to shoot. Many shooters will benefit from them, but shooting as it was will be the loser.

Just one more point on this slightly contentious subject. Undoubtedly one of the most dangerous shooters I ever came across was a man who had just passed his DSC1. To be honest, I wouldn't want to be in the same parish as him if he had a gun or rifle in his hand. I have met others nearly as, but they hadn't spent a lot of money getting to the same stage as the qualification holder!

But I digress. Snares and traps can be a 24-hour weapon in the keeper's arsenal – but for those just wishing to 'have a go' they present quite a few problems. First, there's the time required to check snares a couple of times a day. You also need to spend time locating the best places to drop your wires, and have a fair amount of practice in doing so.

Having said all of this, should you master the craft it can be a very good method of controlling fox numbers. Sadly, today there are more and more non-country people in the country; many of these would certainly not approve of coming across a fox slung up in a snare. There is also the growing possibility of catching one of the large number of dogs that seem to be allowed to run wild. Owners of these will not be impressed if one ends up in a wire, fitted with a stop or not.

For those wishing to try their hand at snaring for the first time, there are a few tips I can pass on. As I said earlier, snares are at work every hour of every day. As well as an advantage, this is a responsibility. The countryside is becoming a busier

place, and there are many dogs and their owners about. It is best to place snares as far away from other people as possible, and obviously inspect them regularly (in fact this is a legal requirement).

Foxes are creatures of habit, and will follow the same runs that have been used for decades. This instinct is very deep-rooted. I once knew of a hedge where I had snared foxes for years; one day the farmer decided to take it down. For some reason he removed half the hedge, which was a typical high-bank Devon type. The half he removed ended a couple of feet from where the run was. Now, the foxes would have been able to walk around the new end of the hedge – but bizarrely they still stuck to the up-and-over run, and I still caught them there.

Mike's last two gins – one for rabbit, one for rat. They are now wall ornaments only

Again, observation will tell you where your foxes are moving – it is then a question of selecting the best spot. Runs are not difficult to find; when you have located one, look for a narrow spot. If there is no suitable natural anchorage, drive your peg into the ground 18 inches to two feet from the run. Set your snare with a 10-inch loop and 10-12 inches off the ground, and hold it firmly in place with a wire or hazel tealer. Do not anchor your wire to a log or a fence line, and do not set your wire any lower than 9-10 inches – you may end up catching other species.

If the spot you wish to set your wire is a wide track unused by passers-by, you can funnel your fox towards it by putting down obstacles such as rocks or sticks. It is possible to catch foxes in new wires that are still shiny, but if you want to dull it down, get some chips of oak bark and boil them up for a while, then when the water is good and brown, put the new snares in and leave them overnight. The tannin will soon stain the wire.

A final word on snares: It will pay anyone setting out on the snaring route for the first time to get a copy of the current laws and guidelines as to what you can and can't do. Be aware – snaring is under intense pressure from those opposed to it, so you must be absolutely sure to keep on the right side of the law.

The number of traps that can now be legally used for foxes is very limited. In the distant past I caught foxes in gins, but thankfully those days are long gone. They were very effective but also very cruel. Today cage traps are the answer, but they are not a sure-fire method of dealing with marauding foxes. To a large extent, the success or failure of a cage trap is down to location. I have never had much success with cage traps in open locations – foxes are far too wary to enter alien objects apart from in extreme circumstances, such as the

advanced stages of mange or a really hard winter. Badgers, on the other hand, will boldly enter where no fox would go. Once trapped, unless the cage is sturdily built, they will wreak havoc on it.

Success with cage trapping, as I said, depends on location and the way the cage merges with the area it is set in. I suppose the best example is in and around poultry. In that situation there is usually a lot of wire netting, corrugated iron and the usual detritus that poultry areas seem to accumulate. In these situations, cage traps can work well, but there are a few rules you will need to follow. Ideally the cage needs to be set alongside a run or fence. I have never noticed any preference for directional facing, but wherever you place the cage, it will need to be left there permanently. Foxes are very quick in noticing changes to the environment they live in.

As far as the size of the trap goes, the bigger the better. One of the most successful ones I ever saw was homemade from heavy weld mesh. It was eight feet long, four feet wide and about four feet high. This was a big old trap – not one you could relocate with ease – so it stayed where it was in the hedge on one side of a poultry yard. Over time the brambles and weed grew around it, and just the entrance was kept clear. Every dead hen or duck was thrown in to the far end of the trap and left.

That trap caught literally hundreds of foxes over the years. It was always set. There are those who say you should leave the door open without setting the release, and the foxes will get used to going in. I don't follow that line of thinking – you only want each fox to go in once, so why get it used to going in and out?

The other method I have had success with is setting a smaller cage trap for the cubs in late summer. I follow the method the American trappers use: put the trap

Right: Set out in the fields, cage traps seldom work, but near coops and runs they can pay dividends

in a black plastic bin liner, then push the trap into thick undergrowth and cover everything visible with the growing herbage, leaving just the entrance open. Soon the growing green stuff will make the trap itself virtually invisible. Cubs are inherently curious – if a rabbit or pretty much anything dead is left inside, it will more often than not attract a curious cub. You could even catch the odd adult, but they are far cannier.

Much is made of keeping your scent away from traps. I am not so sure this is that important, particularly if you are setting in a poultry yard. In fact I am not sure that scent is that important at all whenever you deal with foxes. Unless you live in a remote area with a sparse human population, most foxes will come across human scent all the time and accept it as part of their world.

Wires and cage traps are a proven method of catching foxes, but practice as always makes perfect. Don't forget, there are rules governing the setting of all traps. Whichever type you choose, do check on the current legislation regarding inspection and so on.

There are two other types of trap, which although not specifically set for foxes, have certainly caught them. The obvious one is the Larsen trap used for catching magpies and their cousins. Cubs will infrequently end up in one of these – doubtless to the extreme consternation of the call bird!

The oddest trap I have seen catch cubs was a Kania squirrel trap. These are a small box-type unit with an extremely strong spring arrangement, a little along the lines of a Fenn trap, and they are fixed to the trunk of a tree.

Someone I knew put a Kania low down on a beech tree. Baiting it with peanut butter, he had caught several tree rats, but one morning he went to examine the trap only to find a dead, well grown cub hanging out

likely be looking for a meal. The best bait points in times gone by were the old 'dead pits' on the farms where all the dead stock was dumped. They really pulled every predator in. These, of course, are now illegal.

In the middle of winter with foul weather prevailing, your fox is unlikely to be out in the middle of open, stock-free fields. I say stock-free because I learned many years ago that foxes are drawn to fields where there are sheep, bullocks, horses or any other livestock. I suspect that the presence of stock causes there to be an abundance of beetles, worms, and other invertebrates – together, of course, with such delicacies as afterbirth and stillborn young. When out after foxes all those years ago, the fields with stock were always the most productive, and it was those we always headed to first.

During hard weather, the main factor in choosing my bait points is shelter – both for the fox and for me. Wooded areas are particularly good, as if bad weather sets in it is here the fox will be looking for food – most animals are like us and keep out of the worst of the weather if possible. Many won't have woodland on their ground, so just put yourself in the fox's place and think where you would hunt on a filthy night.

Like cage traps, bait points need to be in place for long periods, and during that time you need to keep a constant supply of bait going. Pretty much anything will do. Many place their faith in things like tins of sardines with a few holes punched in them, others boil up horses' hoof trimmings then leave them in a sealed jar to 'go off'. I have tried many of these along with pretty much everything else, and I wouldn't say I ever really found anything that reliably works better than everything else. Today, someone can read a few tips on the internet, try something once and have a bit of luck, and assume they have struck

of it. Over the next two nights he caught two more, which I guess cleared the litter. They must have really taken a run at it as it was some five feet up the smooth trunk.

There are also bait points. These can be highly effective if you handle them correctly and give a bit of thought to their siting. It is no use putting them just anywhere – you need to think like your local fox and work out where he will most gold. More often than not, it turns out not to be the case.

I, with one exception, stick to rabbit or chicken – corvids seem to be ignored. My one exception is where I am in a temporary situation dealing with a problem fox. At times like this it is not feasible to maintain a 'bait point' in the accepted sense of the word. Here I will use a tin of dog food and mix it with dog biscuits – the small, round type – and scatter it in small amounts in the areas where the fox has been or is expected to be seen and where I can, from a vantage point, see over the area.

Once a fox has picked up the scent and settled down, it will spend time searching over that area for the biscuits. This has worked well for me for a long time, and it's a clean and easy way of carrying some bait with you. If, like me, you happen to live near a poultry farm, these act like a giant bait point, and foxes will be around just about every night.

I normally use either my 4x4 to wait out in, or a high seat. I have found over the past few years that very few foxes take much notice of vehicles. They probably see a vehicle almost every day, and 99 per cent of the time they do them no harm. I sit in the rear passenger seat, being right-handed, and slip a piece of plumbers' insulating foam tube over the window, adjusting it to the right height for the ground I am shooting over. This gives an excellent rest, and I can shoot in comfort. I know it sounds a bit pathetic, but I adjust the radio so it just comes out of the rear speaker and put it on really low. It passes the time on a dark winter's night!

Finally, a few words on driving foxes. Carried out with a bit of planning, this can be a very good way of keeping numbers down. Years ago as a keeper I always organised a few drives after the end of the season – not only did this control numbers,

but it was also thoroughly enjoyable for those who had worked hard during the season, helping out on the shoot, beating and picking up. I employed this method from very early in my foxing life, and always found it not only effective but also a pleasant way of spending some time with like-minded people.

When driving foxes, there are certain rules that must be followed in order to keep things safe. First and foremost, the people involved must really know what they are doing – both the guns and the beaters. The latter will usually have a dog or two. The original 'pack' we used to get

Even the Kania can sometimes catch the odd cub

Once again, knowing your land and the way foxes travel is important. Too many drives are hit-and-miss. When hare coursing was legal, the keepers knew the way the hares would want to travel. Trying to push them the wrong way more often than not just didn't work. It is much easier moving any animal in the direction they instinctively want to go rather than trying to get them to do it your way. This certainly applies to foxes – they know their territory and places of safety, and will usually follow the path they know best.

An example of this was a large wood in the centre of land I shot over. There were always foxes in residence, and it was from here many of them made the short trip to the pig farm I have mentioned elsewhere. Located some half a mile from the cliffs, it was in that direction they would naturally want to go. The problem was that the wood widened at the end nearest the cliffs and was almost impossible to cover effectively.

About 100 yards into the wood at the wide end was an old disused quarry open at both ends. Probably 90 per cent of the foxes passed through it on their way to the cliffs. Once we had realised this, the plan was always the same: a gun was placed at each end of the quarry high above its floor, so shots were taken almost straight down from a height of about 60 feet. Four more guns would cover the far end of the wood, staying out towards its extremities as those foxes that didn't go for the quarry route would head in that direction. Giving the guns time to get into position – there were no mobiles or two-way radios back then – the beating would start.

I always told the guns it was fox only – nothing else was to be shot at. There is nothing worse for a beater than thrashing your way through brambles, blackthorn, mud and mire, hearing shots – which spur the weary body on to even greater efforts –

together comprised about five terriers, a whippet lurcher and a beagle. The latter was absolute mustard on foxes, only failing once in her career. She never knew when to stop! At the end of the day we would have to try to locate her, and more often than not would give up and wait for someone local to find her. Amazingly, always turned up eventually and she never came to any harm.

The dog men and beaters knew their job well and were totally reliable. You don't necessarily need dogs – foxes will move forward easily enough with just a few beaters – but the sound of the dogs when they pick up a scent really gets the nerves and senses tingling.

More important was the selection of the guns. When driving foxes towards the guns, there is clearly a potential for accidents to happen, particularly when a fox is on the move. The guns have to be given clear instructions, and stick to them no matter what.

At the ready: Mike waits out with the rifle by a bait point

only to find that some bright individual had been shooting at pigeons. Trust me – this would only happen once!

The drive would take about half an hour, and it was rare not to pick up two or three each time. The best we managed was seven, and on that occasion even more slipped away.

I enjoy using dogs when driving foxes, but a good team of beaters who know their job they can do equally as well. The secret here is to proceed very slowly, there is no need to make a noise the fox will know you are there the moment you enter the wood, guns need to be in position early and with a minimum of noise.

How you sort your drive will vary depending on the land. If there are isolated patches of cover surrounded by open land, a reliable rifle shot can be placed well out

from the driving area to mop up any that slip away. Overall, fox driving can be efficient, excellent sport, but as always when people, dogs and guns are put into the mix, you must take great care, and the people you involve must understand exactly what their role is. Driving can be both effective and enjoyable, but always take care.

I have deliberately left out working foxes underground with dogs – terriers and lurchers in particular. I have done this type of control in the past, but my knowledge is not enough to advise others how to do it. Furthermore, current legislation for hunting with hounds and lurchers isn't precise, and one could easily fall foul of the law. This also applies to terrier work below ground. Nevertheless, foxing with terriers and lurchers is still an effective form of control practised by a few experts in their own field.

The guns have a well-deserved warm-up after a winter's fox drive

CONTENTIOUS ISSUES

My interest in my early days, as far as shooting and snaring foxes was concerned, was almost exclusively financial. Today, to admit such an interest would be expected to bring forth howls of abuse. Fancy anyone killing things to make money! It was different then – those in the countryside were left alone to do what they wanted. In fact it may seem a strange thing to say today, but in my village 40 years ago, the vast majority of residents were local and knew the ways of the countryside. Today it has changed. Owing to the desirability of many country locations, a lot of people have moved in from towns and cities, paying inflated prices and pushing the cost of living in such places beyond the reach of the locals.

I am all for people being able to live where they want, but with the proviso that they don't interfere with things that go on in that vicinity, and have done for a very long time. Sadly in the country this doesn't seem to happen. Foxes and badgers are a very good example. I can understand those who wish, for the first time in their lives to watch animals on their little patch. That's fine, but don't put down excessive quantities of feed for them – in the long term this does neither the animals nor the local inhabitants any favours. The foxes and badgers become reliant on this readily obtainable source of food, and make it their business to constantly hang around the area, in the process losing their inherent fear of man. This will inevitably bring them into conflict with the local poultry keepers and anyone who has any form of livestock that the fox sees as part of his diet. Over the last 20 years or so, the calls for me to deal with troublesome foxes have increased at a remarkable rate, down in no small part to feeding by humans.

When I first moved here it was relatively uncommon to see a fox around the village. There were a lot in the surrounding areas, but they kept away from habitation, and should you happen across one during daylight hours it would be off in a flash. How things have changed! Now it is common to see foxes at just about any time of day, sunning themselves on the hillsides or wandering around the village surrounds at will. If they chance upon a free meal they will not waste the opportunity, and once again I am called in to deal with the situation. This has a knock-on effect, for the fox feeders look upon the 'tame' fox as theirs, which it clearly isn't, and there can be a bit of an issue between those whose property has been taken and those who like to see 'their' foxes in their gardens.

When I did my first stint as a keeper back in the early 1970s I can't remember having any problems with vermin control of all sorts and the general public – in fact many went out of their way to let me know where foxes had been seen. When I entered the keepering arena for the second time some 30 years later, things had changed, and not for the better. There were a large number of people totally opposed to shooting of all

sorts, and pheasant shooting in particular. Those who had bought property near the shoot complained about their gardens and the damage the pheasants were doing. They complained if a gun was let off within earshot. They phoned the police on a regular basis if we were out after rabbits or foxes at night, and so it went on until it soured the whole thing.

When I first went keepering, the rearing field took priority over everything else. Rearing birds under broody hens was rewarding but very time-consuming and a lot of work. Above all they were vulnerable to fox attacks; my work was, obviously, to tend their needs and keep them safe.

Releasing birds into the pen at six weeks carries similar responsibility but removes a great deal of work; at the same time, a pen full of plump poults acts like a fast-food takeaway for every predator in the area.

It isn't just foxes either. Badgers have always been a problem, but I did have an electric fence as the first line of defence against them and against foxes. I was fortunate in that I never had a bad attack from either of these predators, but they certainly kept you on your toes. Badgers were, and still are, abundant in my part of the world; foxes were also very plentiful, but these you could do something about, so I did. Snares and the rifle were the methods

Mike in his keepering days, checking the sorghum cover crop

with them, attractive creatures they may be. A fox in good condition with the sun on its back is a handsome sight indeed, but that doesn't change the fact that they are predators and very good ones at that. Some are smarter than others, and they do need to be got rid of.

A keeper friend of mine had two disastrous experiences in the space of a couple of weeks, the first when he had a thousand poults for one of his out pens. The usual work had gone into preparation, and everything was ready. It was a large pen with a lot of undergrowth at one end; he had run the dogs through it the night before the poults arrived and shut everything up. During the night a badger had decided to dig into the pen at the end where there was a lot of cover. The birds were released quietly into the pen and left to settle for a few hours. Upon his return a scene of total carnage met his eyes. The badger had killed dozens of the poults then let himself out. If that wasn't bad enough, about three weeks later an enterprising fox managed to go over the top and killed almost 150 poults. That one wasn't as bright as the badger as it was still in there when the keeper returned. It didn't have long to reflect on its misdeeds as retribution was swift and final.

The keeper cannot just leave foxes alone – they have to be controlled. When keepering I really set about them with a will, but no matter how good you may be, there will always be some left, and they all present a threat. Many more people are becoming involved with foxes one way and another these days, owing mainly, I suspect, to television and the aforementioned craze for feeding them. We have all seen the various programmes on urban foxes, and although I have had little experience of them myself, I know quite a few people who have. Without a doubt they are a downright pest, and they increasingly problems by

of choice, and while the former would be working 24 hours a day 365 days a year, the rifle was out night after night, firstly using the traditional lamp, then early night vision as it came into play.

I am a huge fan of night vision. Used properly, it can certainly improve the chances of dealing with foxes. As a keeper I was not selective when it came to dealing

way of disease, disturbance and – probably the most worrying – the odd attack on small children and babies. A friend of mine who lives in London has foxes in their garden on a regular basis – they have actually walked into the house more than once. Many in these areas are becoming increasingly worried by this increasingly bold behaviour. But there are still others who don't want a single fox harmed.

Whether it is past or present, there are certain topics that crop up year in and year out whenever shooting people get together. Two of these I have always been interested in: cubs and the lamp-shy fox.

As each year moves into late spring and early summer, for many of those whose quarry is the fox, the question arises: Do we shoot and trap them at this time of year? Many years ago, when I was younger, I really don't remember this question arising, or at least not as stridently as it does today. The reason, of course, is that at this time of year it is breeding time.

Many people's view on this is subjective in that the fox comes out at the top of the 'should I or shouldn't I?' list. I am sure much of this stems from the fact that the fox resembles the country's top pet, the dog, and that it is quite large and attractive to look at.

Certainly I go along with those thoughts – without a doubt it is an attractive animal and its young are nice to look at. But that

The village: Situated in typical Devon landscape, this is ideal fox country

also applies to some of our other native species. To many people, baby rabbits are also cute and cuddly. But the fact that many rabbits are killed all year round while breeding doesn't seem to take up much headline space. Countless pigeons are shot throughout the summer, yet how many people search the hedgerows looking for orphaned squabs?

That the fate of young cubs causes much consternation is understandable, yet what is the answer, if indeed there is one? Of course, the obvious one is to leave them alone during the breeding season. Indeed, some advocate a close season as they do with pigeons, and I have even heard this request where rabbits are concerned.

The problem, particularly where the fox is concerned, is that it is probably at its most destructive during and just after the breeding season. This is totally understandable as the parents have to provide for, in some cases, multiple mouths. More and more I see and hear evidence of large litters – the biggest I saw last year was seven, and seven cubs take a bit of feeding. For busy parents, lambs and poultry are also at their most available and vulnerable at this time, and that's where the problem lies.

There are those who say all fox control should be over and done with by the end of the old year. Years ago this was perhaps more feasible than it is today, with hunts, many more professional keepers and the fact that winter fox skins could make really good money. Today we have the Hunting Act, far fewer keepers, no market for fox fur, and a massive growth in the number of urban foxes, many of whom seem miraculously to turn up in the countryside. Contrary to what some may say, not all of these 'transported' animals succumb to shot or starvation. And, of course, there are many now living in the countryside who

actively support the fox population by feeding them.

Despite the growing number of fox shooters who actively pursue the new sport of foxing, the numbers of foxes, in my area anyway, are on the increase. With this increase comes more of the larger litters mentioned earlier. Personally I try to account for as many foxes that are causing problems as I can, and I suppose I do reasonably well. However, when I add up the number of litters that I assume or know are in my area, I realise I am constantly running up the down escalator.

So what is the answer? I don't think there is a clear one. In the country most people have the welfare of animals, tame or wild, at heart and wouldn't deliberately set out to cause suffering. Where this line of thought comes to a shuddering halt is when the farmer finds grown lambs killed or injured, requiring vet's bills, and the smallholder or poultry keeper finds carnage among the flock by day or night. In situations where someone's livelihood may be at stake, the predation clearly has to be stopped, no matter what the consequences may be.

Returning to the idea of the close season, the line of thinking here is that the cubs can be cleared up at harvest time, thereby getting the numbers back to normal. All well and good, but – and it's a very big but – in reality how many cubs of the new season's crop are you going to account for? Certainly a lot get killed on the roads and by the gun. Yet with what appears to be increasingly large litters and the basic fact that few actually know how many foxes there are on their land, the harvest-time cull is really a non-starter. From my own observations in an area I know very well, and spend all my days on and around it, fox numbers are growing.

So what of the cubs if the vixen or dog is shot at breeding time – is it all doom and

Do we need a close season for vixens? Not necessarily – it may do more harm than good

88 A FOXING LIFE WITH GUN AND RIFLE

*Above: The cubs are more able to survive without the vixen than you might think
Right: Foxing the classic way, with lamp and rifle*

gloom? I don't think so. Obviously some will starve, but this also applies to the young of foxes killed on the roads. Many, however, don't die. The most vulnerable are the newly born who are totally reliant on the vixen – if deprived of her milk there is no substitute and they will quickly slip away.

Incidentally, I don't think too many vixens are killed at this stage as she will not travel far from the den while the cubs are suckling. As they grow and start taking solids, the dog fox has a role to play, and should the vixen be killed at this stage he will continue to feed the young. It has also been reported in various studies that others in the family group will take over the feeding of orphaned cubs. I have no personal knowledge of this but apparently it happens.

So the final choice as to whether to squeeze the trigger at this time of year when you have a fox in your sights remains your choice. Remember that not all the foxes you see will have litters.

One thing is for sure. If your local farmer, smallholder or poultry keeper finds their stock mutilated, dead and dying, it is unlikely they will follow your point of view if you say you can't do anything about it because of the cubs! Especially as the cubs will follow exactly the same path next

year. At the end of the day it is a question of conscience tempered by reality and common sense.

The other facet of fox shooting that crops up constantly when fox shooters meet is lamp-shy foxes. I have little doubt that such animals exist, but I am equally sure there are not as many as some people think. In times gone by, when lamping foxes was in its infancy I have no doubt that many foxes really were lamp-shy. The countryside was dark, few lights were seen, and cars were few and far between, so the sudden appearance of a bright light would have been the signal for a rapid departure. Gradually we learned how to get round this by a variety of means, such as not shining the lamp directly on the fox, by keeping its natural curiosity focused on small squeaks, and moving extremely slowly and silently. It didn't always work, but enough were fooled to ensure we got the numbers we needed.

Today things are totally different. Wherever you go in the countryside there are lights – they are everywhere. Cars, travelling at all hours through the country lanes, farm vehicles working into the small hours, 4x4 vehicles charging round the fields, security lights – the list goes on and on. Light pollution is becoming a real problem – even the fairly innocent activity of looking at the stars is now confined to a few special sites not yet ruined by lights. Even the humble glow-worm is in severe decline, because the lovelorn male cannot detect the radiant bride-to-be amid the welter of manmade light.

This sounds a bit dramatic, but those who use night vision will be well aware of the constant lights picked up in their NV devices. There are still dark areas where things remain much as they were, but generally speaking, the nights are not without lights. This raises the question:

Why should the average fox, which will see lights of one sort or another most nights of its life, be lamp-shy? I suspect that although light may have a small bearing on their behaviour, it is what is behind the light that causes them most worry. Many nocturnal animals' reaction to lights at night is often predictable: rabbits, for example, will run to the hedge when lamped from a vehicle, and stop. I would imagine that a very high percentage of rabbits that are shot end their days at the foot of the hedge, where if they had taken just one or two more steps they would have been safe.

A fox's reactions are far more difficult to predict as they are far more individualistic than most of our native species. One thing they have in common with most predators is a high degree of curiosity. Spend some time watching a fox as it roams the fields, and it has its nose into everything – each sound is analysed and every scent investigated. This behaviour can be clearly seen in daylight, and now with night vision it can be watched at night.

On many occasions I have been waiting in a high seat for a particular fox to show up and have spotted lampers in action over the boundary after fox or rabbit. More than once I have been watching a fox on that land when the lampers arrive. Immediately, the fox knows they are there – no matter how skilful we may think we are, the finely honed senses of the fox are light years ahead of ours, and he straight away knows there is possible danger.

Watching a fox in these circumstances can be very informative. Sometimes they carry on as if nothing untoward is happening, at other times they make an extremely rapid exit, but the most common reaction is curiosity. On several occasions when out and about I have noticed the same fox following me night after night. I guess that once they have ascertained that

Out foxing on the stubbles – no evidence of lamp-shy foxes tonight!

Traditional kit: A lamping rig from the early days

there are humans about, provided they feel in control, they will keep a watching brief on proceedings.

Like most animals, foxes rely mainly on three senses to warn them of danger: sight, smell and hearing. From what I have seen, in most cases they need confirmation of two of these before deciding on the next course of action. Deer exhibit this very well indeed. I used to go to some land where there was always a good head of fallow. Moving with the wind in my face, it was quite common to get within sight of a group of them. Often I would watch them for a while and carry out a few amateurish experiments to test my two-out-of-three theory. They had no idea I was there, so I would start with a 'clean sheet'. The first time I whistled at them (they were about 50 yards away), heads instantly went up and they got a bit restless. After a few minutes they settled down again and carried on as normal. The next time I found them, the same thing happened, only this time I was behind a tree. Without totally revealing myself, I waved an arm at them (I did say it was amateurish). Again the heads were up, staring in my direction, but as I made no further moves they soon settled. Some time later I found a group in a situation that allowed me to work round them so that my scent was carried to them, but at

no time did I make a noise or show myself – same result.

The last bit of the experiment was to do two of the items together. Make a sound and then show myself, get my scent to them and snap a twig, and finally give them a visual followed by a sound. Each time they would be gone in a flash. This is the same behaviour shown more often than not by plains game in Africa. Animals instinctively know that to run blindly at the first sign of danger can be fatal, as they may be running into danger rather than away from it. So it is with the fox.

When we walk into a field with lamp and gun in hand, the fox almost always knows we are there, alerted by sound, sight or smell. But it is quite possible it is not exactly sure where the danger lies. Suddenly a light illuminates the night, he has confirmation of danger and where it lies, and he is gone.

When moving into a field where you suspect a fox may be, it will pay to wait a while before flicking the light on – let its initial suspicions subside before carrying on as usual. There will always be exceptions to every rule – there will be foxes that will flee at the first sign of a light or a sound – but I suspect, more often than not, that by the time the light goes on they are well aware you are there. This can be borne out by the number of foxes you will pick up in the lamp at a fair distance away, say 100 yards or more, that will just stare back at you. The light, in that case, will have been the first sign of danger. If you then move or your scent gets to them, in most cases they will be gone. Once you realise the way a fox reacts, you can use this in your favour. It doesn't always work, but it helps.

These two issues, cubs and the lamp shy fox, are very unlikely ever to be completely laid to rest. Much will depend on your own attitude and how imperative it is to remove foxes from your area.

Foxing partnership: The keeper and his reliable fox-killing labrador Talon

FOXES I HAVE KNOWN

I've already covered a few instances when, despite the best efforts of the owner or keeper, a fox or foxes have gained entrance to runs, coops or pens and have wreaked havoc inside. When I was keepering I was fortunate never to have had a fox get inside any of the release pens. I did have buzzards, though – today this raptor is probably as big a threat to some keepers as the fox. Compared with a fox, a bird is pretty unpredictable, and where our raptors are concerned, apart from trying to keep them away (almost impossible) there is nothing you can do.

In my first stint as a keeper, however, there was plenty you could do – mainly shoot them. Having said that, few of the keepers I knew back then were inclined to spend hours traipsing round the shoot hoping to see a buzzard, sparrowhawk or tawny owl – but if there was one round the pen, it would be dealt with. Now that makes sense to me – people should be able to protect their property. Today a keeper shooting a buzzard would be punished more severely than some hooded youth beating up an old lady – it really doesn't make sense to me.

One of the worst cases of pheasant poult destruction I ever came across was where, the night before the poults arrived, a badger dug its way into the pen. It was still there, unbeknown to the keeper, early the following morning when the poults were released. As usual after release, the poults were left well alone to settle in. Returning at midday, he was faced with total carnage. The badger had killed dozens of poults, and the rest were totally traumatised. After the killing was over it let itself out by ripping a hole in the wire netting.

Foxes, of course, don't possess the same power as badgers, but they are remarkably persistent when trying to get into a pen. I was once approached by a lady who kept a lot of poultry and ducks. Despite taking great care, she suffered fox attacks year after year, particularly at cub time. This time it was her ducks that had been selected. There was a stream running through her land, and at some point a large pond had been dug. It was now overgrown with scrub and general weed growth. Somehow a fox had got in and out, in the process taking one and killing another half-dozen or so. Surrounding the pond area was a seven-foot-high plastic-covered chain link fence with the top covered by netting. Considerable attention had been paid to setting the fencing into the ground, and all in all one would have said it was fox-proof.

I searched for signs of digging underneath the fence, checked the barricades where the stream ran through the compound, but to no avail. A couple of nights later there was a repeat visit with yet more ducks killed. Clearly there was a weak point, so I went over for another search. Going round the pen for the second time, I paid more attention to the lower side where there was a lot more undergrowth.

Spotting signs of a slightly defined run into the long grass and nettles, I found it. I was more than surprised to find the fox had bitten through the chain-link fencing. Now this was not cheap stuff – it had been reclaimed from a tennis court and was in excellent condition, yet the fox had clearly bitten through enough of the links to allow it to get through.

After a bit of surveillance work I found an earth with well grown cubs a few hundred yards away on neighbouring land – land where foxes couldn't be shot. No more visits occurred, and there was no sign of the fox for a couple of weeks. Then the smallholder rang to say the fox had been trying to open up the repaired hole in the pen.

Returning that evening, I set myself up for a long wait. I was using the Archer night vision, an excellent unit that has served me well for years, and had positioned myself in the hedge, which gave a good view across the small paddock leading to the pen. As the last of the late evening light faded, the sound of a blackbird's fox/cat warning "pink, pink" got me on the alert. Sure enough, a few moments later a small fox trotted purposefully across the grass towards the pen. Clearly familiar with the set-up, it knew exactly where it was going. It paused for a moment before

through that level of discomfort merely to get at the ducks was a mystery.

As a follow-on from this event, years later the lady with the ducks phoned to say something had been trying to get into the pen again. At the old entry point there were clear signs of something chewing on the link fencing. A few nights later I accounted for a dog fox. Not only did this happen on that occasion, it happened again a while later. I assume these foxes must have visited the duck pen with the vixen when they were cubs, copying the behaviour of their mother. After the second fox was accounted for, the trouble ceased.

I remember another fox that used extreme ingenuity to gain access to some poultry, this time a big old dog. Again this was a smallholding where the owner had spent a lot of time, money and effort ensuring her valuable collection of pure-bred poultry was well protected. Despite this, a fox had got into the run and killed a dozen or so birds. The usual search for the entry route revealed absolutely nothing – not a sign. I said I would come back when time allowed, but I heard nothing more for a week. Then another phone call and another visit. Same result – nothing. I even tried using trail cameras, but they revealed nothing. This state of affairs continued for a few weeks – and it always happened on a Tuesday night. This was too much of a coincidence to ignore, and by now I had taken on this fox as a bit of a personal challenge.

Having searched the outside perimeter several times without any joy, I tried a change of tactics. I made a thorough search, this time inside the huge run, which was at least 100 yards long and nearly as wide. I went round the whole thing with a fine-tooth comb. Eventually I found what appeared to be the exit route. The straining post at one of the corners had scratch marks on it and muddy marks all the way up.

entering the run into the fence, allowing me an easy shot.

The fox was a small vixen in excellent condition considering she had brought up a litter. There was only one thing that marred an otherwise good specimen: her teeth. Unsurprisingly, although I would have put her age at around three years old, most of her rear molars were completely worn away. Why an animal should have gone

Also, there were a couple of white chicken feathers caught in the wire. This had to be where it was getting out. But it certainly couldn't get in the same way – and this still didn't explain why it always seemed to happen on a Tuesday night.

The following Wednesday morning I drove over and parked outside the house. This is an old farmhouse typical of this area, where the outside wall of the house runs alongside the road and forms part of a high wall that runs the length of the property. Parking up against the wheelie bins, I got out into a grey winter's morning, damp and miserable. Walking towards the entrance, I happened to glance at the light green wheelie bin and saw cat tracks on top. Or were they? Closer inspection showed them to be fox pad marks, etched in mud and still fresh. The next marks were on the tiled top of the wall some three feet above

the wheelie bin. A quick trip through the gate and into the yard soon revealed more muddy pad marks on top of a corrugated tin roof, the other side of the wall from the wheelie bin. From there it was a six-foot jump into the run. Easy when you knew how it was done. It had been trying to dig into one of the coops, this time without success, and fresh muddy footprints were clearly visible on the exit fence pole.

This fox had worked out that a wheelie bin out on the road allowed it to gain access to the feast inside. I don't suppose for a moment that it set out to do this – more than likely it was trying to get into the wheelie bin itself in the first place, and things just progressed from there.

Personally given the resourcefulness of this particular fox, I would have suggested re-siting the bin, as that would have solved the problem. However, the owner of the

Fowl play: Ducks can be easy prey for foxes

out, that was a massive understatement. I had always been told that foxes loved pig meat, but foxes taking small piglets was something I had no personal experience of.

The first night we arrived at the farm, we were given directions to the rearing field – it was only a couple of hundred yards from the farmhouse so we were soon going through the gate into the field. Putting the lamp round the five or so acres revealed something I hadn't seen before and certainly haven't since. There were fox eyes shining back out of the darkness from every direction. At a guess, there must have been a couple of dozen.

The farm was situated in a heavily wooded area and was only about half a mile from the sea, which was fringed with cliffs covered in gorse and scrub. It was also running with rabbits – all in all, it was ideal fox country. Nobody shot there in those days, and it was avoided by the hunt because of the cliffs. I don't suppose there were more than a couple of foxes killed here every year. The fox population must have been huge.

The foxes were clearly used to seeing lights around the rearing field as the farmer checked the sows and litters every few hours throughout the night. He said he had seen the odd fox, but as he only used a hand torch it wasn't surprising he didn't see the numbers we saw that first night.

As we only used shotguns then, some care had to be exercised not to add to the dead pig tally. What we couldn't understand was how the foxes were getting the very young piglets with the sow in attendance, as they are very protective of their young. As we were new to the ground we were a bit handicapped that first night, and only managed to shoot a couple of the many foxes we saw. A good look round the next day revealed fox runs and other signs of them everywhere.

chickens was adamant that the fox had to go, so the following Tuesday night I waited out with the night vision. Shortly after dark a large dog fox trailed across the back field and headed directly towards the bin. A quick shot stopped it, and that was that. From then on the wheelie bin was parked across the other side of the road and there were no more visits into the run. I assume the fox I shot was the culprit, but you can never really be sure. Whatever the case, this was one resourceful fox. Clearly it didn't know the days of the week, but it went to prove once more that they are always around, always looking for the opportunity for an easy meal.

Foxes are resourceful creatures and will soon spot an opportunity where food is concerned. Many years ago there was a farm where pigs were bred; these were farrowed in arks spread across a large field. The owner noticed one day that piglets seemed to be going missing, and got in touch to say he suspected it might be a fox. As it turned

The fox that chewed its way through chain link fencing. It shows the lengths foxes will go to

We returned a couple of nights later, and the farmer said he would keep away so as not to complicate matters. It soon became clear how the foxes were getting the newly born piglets. Firstly, they seemed to be working in twos or threes. One would jump up on the ark roof and lay looking down over the entrance, then one or two others would go right up to the entrance of the ark. Eventually the sow would come out to drive off the intruders, at which point the fox on the roof would jump down and in a flash be in the ark and out with one of the youngsters. There seemed to be at least three 'teams' working this system at the same time – something I have never seen since.

As shooting among the arks themselves was difficult, not to mention disturbing to the sows, we decided to get them on the way to the rearing field. We also laid a considerable number of snares in the well used runs. In the course of the following three weeks or so we must have accounted for something like 50 foxes, and the piglet problem all but disappeared. I have no idea as to how many new-born pigs had been taken, but it must have been substantial. Certainly the foxes had worked out a very good strategy for getting what they wanted. What I found most interesting was that several seemed to be using the same system – so they must have had a fair bit of practice.

Sometimes when called to deal with fox problems, things can work out really well, even profitably. In my early days of setting up a fox control business, a lady called and said she had been losing some of her pedigree cats. She lived in a very affluent part of Torquay looking out over the sea – a spectacular spot, and as it was so close to the cliffs, foxes were certainly there as they like this sort of terrain. Plenty of cover and wildlife, but also the chance of some easy pickings around the houses at night.

The lady told me that she had seen a big fox pick up one of the kittens that morning, bringing the tally to four. While I am no cat lover, I could understand the lady's feelings, so I said I would head over later in the morning to have a look round. Arriving at the beautiful house and going into the garden, I saw the lady doing some weeding among the flower beds. I had my big lurcher Sam with me. I'd also brought the gun – I had been caught out before when I'd gone to see a job, stumbling across a fox and having nothing with me in the way of tools.

Top: Foxes will eat every part of a bird, but sometimes the feet are left behind
Above: A head a fox has left behind. Usually it is eaten

A quick chat to the pleasant but rather upset lady had her pointing out where the fox usually came into the garden. This was the edge of the lawn, which dropped down steeply to the road, the other side of which was rough ground running down to the cliffs. The distance from where we were talking to the edge of the lawn was about 20 yards, so the dog and I went over to see what we could see. Standing looking out over the sea, I was struck by two things – firstly the wonderful view and how nice it must be to have loads of money, and secondly the fact that my dog was sitting in a somewhat rigid position, staring downwards.

Following the direction of his fixed gaze, I realised I was looking at a fox, curled up in a patch of grass looking calmly up at up. It couldn't have take more than a couple of seconds to get a cartridge into the gun, but it seemed to me that it an absolute age, and made a great deal of noise to boot. I expected to see the fox disappear, but fortunately it didn't. Finally the gun was closed, and at 20-odd yards almost straight down, it was a straightforward shot.

I think the lady must have almost had kittens herself on the spot, as the sound of a 12-bore wasn't a common occurrence in this exclusive area. I went over to explain

Above: The fox responsible for this killed about 60 birds before it was caught Left: Safe for now – but the foxer's work never ceases

what had happened, and we were joined after a couple of minutes by Sam, who was carrying a very large dead fox. Sam then disappeared, and returned almost immediately with half a kitten. Proof if it was needed that the job had been done. I supposed mixed emotions was the best way to describe what the lady was going through – the half a kitten would probably have been best left where it was, but the dog was always thorough at what he did!

Composing herself, the lady ushered me inside (just me – not the dog), and pressed me to a large sherry (what else). Asked what she owed – remember, this was the late 1960s – I said 10 pounds. After all, she was clearly very well off, I wasn't, and I had been there all of half an hour. Leaving the room, she returned and gave me not 10 but 50 pounds – an absolute fortune. Probably the most profitable fox control job I ever did. As a gesture of gratitude, I buried the remains of the kitten free of charge. I was such a softie back then.

A couple of unusual fox shooting episodes stick in my mind, both involving cattle. The first was on a little holding in the next village. It was the usual case of a fox raiding the yards for chickens or whatever was there at the time. The owner had a few pigs and two or three small heifers; there was one particularly tame one called Toffee. Toffee could be a blessed nuisance at times when I was there after foxes – she would follow me round like a dog. Not only that – in the summer months she was always accompanied by a cloud of horse flies, which were only too pleased to switch from Toffee to me.

This particular night I had tucked myself away in the hedge with my unwanted friend standing guard. Apart from the haze of biting insects, it was a pleasant enough evening, during which I mostly watched a pair of peregrine falcons working the pigeons that were taking the last of the wheat off the stubbles.

Darkness started to close in, and half an hour later even the excellent Swarovski scope could see no more. Without warning the fox was there, working down the rough hedge bottom on the other side of the field. Within a moment Toffee spotted it and was watching intently. After a moment the fox slipped into a dense patch of reeds and disappeared. Toffee was still watching. Suddenly the fox's head appeared briefly; again it withdrew into the reeds. I could sense this was going to be a dead loss, as by now I could only just make out the reeds. Suddenly Toffee was gone, heading straight

for the reeds. She stood on the edge, staring into their depths, and started throwing her head around. Then, without warning, she charged straight in.

In a flash the fox was out on to the open field, and with just enough light left to see it, the quiet evening was woken up by the sound of the .223. Toffee ambled over and prodded the dead vixen with her head a couple of times, then once again came back

Top: This fox had been running around the wire for days
Above: Hens will sometimes put their head through a wire if a fox runs alongside. Not a good idea

to me. I did contemplate taking her over as a full-time foxing heifer; the problem would have been getting her in the back of the 4x4.

The other cattle moment was when I shot a fox that was crossing a field of cattle, some of which had calves at foot. South Devon cattle are pretty placid as a rule, so what happened next was rather surprising. The fox was about 50 yards from the nearest cow. I shot it, and the cow never moved. A few moments later the cow started roaring, making more noise than any bull I had ever heard. She approached the dead fox and started butting the carcase and even stamping on it. By now the rest of the herd had arrived, attracted by the commotion. The noise was indescribable. Eventually there was basically nothing left of the fox except a red stain on the churned-up grass. People in the village almost a mile away had heard the rumpus, and some had even turned out to see what it was all about.

I imagine that the combination of a predator in the field together with the mother's natural protective instinct, and the fact that for once the cow had actually been able to catch up with a fox, caused her to go haywire. Whatever the cause, it was pretty spectacular, and it's the only time I have ever seen this type of behaviour.

The very worst case of fox damage occurred many years ago on a relatively small poultry farm a few miles from where I live. It comprised three houses, each containing about 400 birds. These were free-range layers, so during the day they had the run of a third of the field each. At dusk they would be shut in for the night.

On this particular occasion birds were shut in as usual, and in the morning it was the children's job to go and let the birds out. Shortly after they ran off they returned in tears, saying something had killed the chickens. The smallholder was soon on

the spot, where a scene of sheer carnage greeted him. A fox, or far more likely foxes, had gained access to the birds through the door, which clearly hadn't been shut properly. Out of the 400 or so birds that were housed there, only half a dozen remained untouched.

The next-door neighbour, who had a digger, dug out a pit, and the birds were collected and buried. The couple who ran the smallholding were so devastated that they sold up and moved away. I have never seen anything like it before or since, but knowing what effective killers foxes can be, I wasn't all that surprised. A fox is more than capable of killing a chicken or pheasant with one quick bite to the neck or across the back – it only takes a moment. The fox is an expert executioner, and nothing they do surprises me any more.

Above: The fox: A more effective killer than even we sometimes realise
Left: These two were after the hens – not any more

RIFLES AND SHOTGUNS

Over the years I have shot foxes with many rifles and shotguns. People often ask, "Which was the best?" In truth there is no clear answer to that question.

As far as rifles go, in my early years I used the humble .22 Long Rifle exclusively. I had no choice, and without any doubt this little calibre is quite capable of killing a fox. The difficulty with the .22LR is that it really doesn't have the knockdown power necessary to drop a fox on the spot every time. What's more, its 'loopy' trajectory can cause problems placing a shot exactly where it's needed. However, I still use a 22LR in certain circumstances. Around buildings is a good example, where you really need to be as quiet as possible, and equipped with a good sound moderator it can do a good job. It is without doubt a close-range calibre, and I limit its use on fox out to a maximum of about 50 yards. Headshots are preferable with this round, although a fox's head is very small, so unless you are confident of placing your shot accurately then heart shooting is the best option.

That, of course, applies to whichever rifle you are using. It has been said so often, but can never be repeated enough, that the aim of any person using a gun or rifle to shoot any living creature should be to ensure it is killed as swiftly and as humanely as possible. Things can always go wrong, but it is our responsibility to minimise that as much as possible.

For many years now, the rifle has largely replaced the shotgun as the tool of choice when after foxes. Huge discussions take place on the various shooting websites as to the best and most suitable calibre for foxing. Having tried quite a lot over the years for my own use and for magazine reviews, the conclusion I have come to is that to a large degree it really doesn't matter. Much more crucial are where you shoot and how good a shot you are.

As far as where you shoot goes, the factors involved are many and varied. Clearly if most of your fox shooting is done around smallholdings, farm buildings or in proximity to dwellings, then a smaller, quieter calibre will suit your needs. You certainly don't want to be blazing away with a .243 if there are houses a few yards away. In these days of double glazing it may be amazing how little people hear of the outside goings on, but for all the hassle it can cause it is generally better to be as inconspicuous as possible.

Looking through the various reloading manuals, I am amazed by the vast number of calibres there are, up to and including the .243. While calibres above this size are often used on foxes, this, I suspect, is more likely to be down to deerstalkers taking the opportunity to roll over a passing fox, as opposed to professional fox controllers. So what does the foxing newcomer go for?

Firstly, be clear on what you will use the rifle for. Are you thinking of getting a rifle purely for foxing, or will deer be on the menu as well? Should the latter be the case then your choice will be made for you

– .243 or above it will have to be to make it deer legal. Should you be someone who will only be shooting the odd fox when out after rabbits, then a good choice could be the .17 HMR or even the new .17 Hornet. Both of these diminutive rounds will take out a fox, the first out to about 100 yards, the second almost double that.

My experience of the .17 Hornet is that as an occasional long-range accurate vermin round it's fine, but should you require the rabbit to eat then the .17 HMR will undoubtedly do far less damage to the carcase. While I was quite taken with the .17 Hornet, my gut feeling was that it was neither fish nor fowl. Unless you wanted a rifle solely for long-range vermin control, it was hard to see where it fitted in.

Another round that was much used in my youth was the .22 Hornet. It has been going a very long time, and is reasonably easy to reload. I like this round but it does have its limitations. Although it will drop a fox in its tracks at 200 yards, you really

Mike with the .22LR – a calibre perfectly capable of dispatching foxes

do have to know your rifle well at this sort of range, as the trajectory is fairly pronounced compared to other, more modern calibres. As a boy I had a keeper friend who used a Hornet for everything. I once saw him drop a fallow buck stone dead at just short of 100 yards. My own .22 Hornet gives me considerable pleasure on the occasions I use it, but in truth there are better fox rounds available.

Moving up in size, we come to what I consider the classic pure fox rounds: the .222, the .223 and finally the .22-250. Over the past 20 years or so I have moved my fox rifle allegiance to the .223. There was no particular reason for this except perhaps that I found the .22-250 a bit on the loud side. The .222 undoubtedly has legions of followers, but it dropped into my 'why' category (as opposed to the ever-tempting 'why not'). If you own a .223 you will have no difficulty obtaining factory ammunition for it, and if you follow the reloading route I have found it one of the easier rounds to load.

The techies out there will give all sorts of reasons why this, that or the other calibre is better than any other, citing ballistic properties out to 300 yards or so. My take is this: I have shot many thousands of foxes in my life, and for many years, kept a record of the ranges most of them were taken at. The average always worked out pretty much the same: around 100 yards. I am no long-range shooter, particularly at night – I think the longest I have ever shot was around the 250-yard mark, and that was exceptional for me. I would far rather wait and get the fox closer, or work my way out to it and get the range down to as short as possible. I will achieve guaranteed kills on far more foxes at 100 yards that I will at twice that distance. I know a few shooters who are really good shots and are more than capable of hitting small targets

out to 300 yards or further, but these are, in my opinion, rare birds. Most of us mere mortals are nowhere as good as this, so bearing in mind my mantra about clean kills, I shall always be, on average, a 100-yard man.

Referring again to the internet, newcomers should be aware that there are often some extraordinarily wild claims made on forums relating to people's prowess with a rifle, particularly at night. Some claim to drop foxes on a regular

Left: Concealment and, above all, patience will get you the results you desire
Above: The HMR round (top) dealt with this fox

basis, at night, out to 400 yards. I have seen a lot of fox eyes at that sort of range, and that's about it – just eyes. It is highly dangerous, in my opinion, to be shooting at eye reflection at that sort of range. I have heard some horror stories of near disasters where people have relied on just eye shine to take a shot. In fact in my own part of the world, some years back there was the worst of all disasters when a member of a lamping party ended up being shot dead. I think the shot was taken at what was thought to be a pair of fox eyes.

I was also told the story of a couple of chaps out lamping who saw eyes reflecting back at the foot of a hedge. Deciding to take the shot, the rifleman clearly hit the target, and the pair made their way to pick up the fox. As they approached they heard groaning coming from the other side of the hedge where there was a lane. Fearing the worst, they made their way round to the lane where they came across a body stretched out on the ground, alive but groaning and moaning. Horrified, they assumed he had been shot; it soon became apparent that he was just drunk. So had they shot at? Clutched in the paralytic man's hand was a dog lead, and on the end of it, a dead corgi.

Having now got over their initial shock and realising that a murder charge had been avoided, the pair turned their attentions to the dead dog. The man was so drunk he had all but passed out, took off the dog's collar, removed the corgi, and re-assembled the lead and collar. The dog was later buried and the owner presumably thought the dog had just run off.

Whether or not it is actually true, this tale brings home just how careful you need to be when shooting at night. As more and more people take to covert night shooting with night vision, showing no light, the need to take care will only increase. The thought of an accident involving another human is too horrific to contemplate.

So my choice of calibre would be .223 if the rifle is to be used exclusively for fox, and probably .243 if roe is on the agenda as well. With both of these rounds I, in common with many others, zero about half an inch high at 100 yards. This allows shots to be taken out to 200 yards with no allowance for drop.

When the choice of calibre has been decided upon, perhaps the next thing that causes much discussion is what make and model to get. I have tested and reviewed many makes, and to be perfectly honest, today there are no really bad rifles. A degree of accuracy suitable for shooting a fox is more or less built in as standard these days. In the media and online, there's much discussion of how much more accurate this make is than the other. This might be important if you are a target shooter; I am not, though I did shoot competition in the RAF. All I want is a rifle that will hit and kill a fox humanely. I think of the target area of a fox as similar in size to a beer mat or a clay pigeon. If you can consistently hit either of these at 100 yards then you will be fine on a fox. Most modern rifles will do that reliably.

Nevertheless, newcomers often press me to suggest a make of rifle to buy, because the more they delve into the matter and the more advice they get, the harder it becomes for them to make a reasoned decision as to the best choice. As I have said before, the internet can be hugely confusing – it is quite natural for people to have varying views, and on shooting forums, all these views are aired in one place.

If you were to pin me down, my advice would be look at some reviews, get a few catalogues, go and look around your local gun shop, pick up a few prospective new firearms and get a feel for it. To start with,

The .22 Hornet can be an effective fox round out to nearly 200 yards

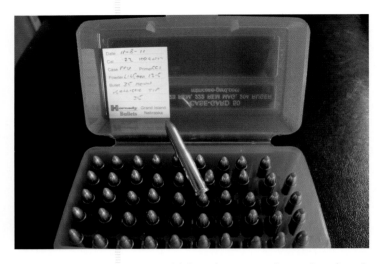

Above: Reloads for the .22 Hornet
Above right: Testing a semi-auto at the local clay ground

I would largely ignore the make of each rifle you consider. So many factors come into the choice of a rifle – price is only the beginning. Do you like wood or do you prefer a synthetic stock? The latter has the advantage of not being susceptible to weather or moisture changes, so there is no movement of the stock and forend, which can happen with a rifle with woodwork. Having said that, I can't say it has ever proved a problem for me. I like the feel and appearance of the natural material, but it can get damaged when out in the field – something that really shouldn't happen to synthetic stocks.

If you have a friend who shoots, ask him what he thinks. Retain your own critical judgement, though. We all like to think our make and calibre of rifle is the best, and there is nothing particularly wrong with that. But when setting out to get your first rifle, hearing all these opinions can be highly confusing.

As I have said, the inaccurate rifle is pretty much a thing of the past, so whichever you choose, I would like to think you won't go too far wrong. Having said that, I once had a rifle made by a highly respected maker – one that is

highly popular – and it didn't shoot well at all. In the end the factory exchanged it for another, and the replacement worked just fine. In my experience, this is extremely unusual – today it is very rare for any rifle, particularly a centrefire, not to shoot well straight from the box. I am excluding custom rifles from these comments, as I suspect few newcomers would go down that route to start with.

Another couple of factors to bear in mind are resale value and the cost of running your rifle. As with most things in this day and age, if you buy new it is highly unlikely your rifle will appreciate in value. And it is the way of the human hobbyist that he seldom sticks with whatever he starts off with. I suspect that most shooters change their rifles more often than they would like to admit to. I can look back over many things in my life that I have changed, often just for the sake of it, and with hindsight I know I probably would have done just as well to stick with the original. I would certainly have saved a considerable amount of money. However, I would have missed out on a lot of anticipation and enjoyment, so I guess we have to live with our weaknesses.

So when, almost inevitably, you go to change your rifle for the next one, you will probably get a nasty shock as to the price you are offered. Trade-ins will always get you more from a dealer, but the best price will be obtained if you can sell privately. Many rifles change hands this way, particularly over the internet; the downside that you have little back-up if things go wrong. It's fair to say, though, that many such deals go through without a hitch.

The drop in price will obviously be greater if you buy new from a dealer, so perhaps a second-hand rifle from the same source might be worth considering

for your first buy. If, in due course, you decide to change it, your loss will be substantially less.

In the case of a first buy, remember, match your rifle to its purpose. Remember also that licensing laws may govern your choice – they are interpreted differently by the various authorities, so it may do no harm to check the suitability of your choice of rifle with them. As time goes by, you may wish to diversify into other calibres – but by then you will know a lot more about the whole rifle scene.

All my rifles are fitted with sound moderators of a variety of makes. I would suggest that all foxing rifles be fitted with a mod, not only for reducing the sound of

the shot but also for the other function they carry out: diffusing the sound of the shot, masking the direction it came from. On more than one occasion I have shot at a fox positioned against a hedge and missed, only to have it run straight towards me as it has heard the shot strike the hedge rather than the sound of the shot.

Again, just about all sound moderators will do the job. Some certainly reduce sound more than others, but that is not the be all and end all of the debate. There are so many variables when shooting in the field, terrain and wind being the most noticeable, meaning it really is a matter of personal choice for the newcomer. I have four different makes of sound moderators

in constant use, ranging from an expensive Quicksilver titanium model to one of the Wildcat range. To be honest, I have never noticed much of a difference in how wildlife reacts to all four.

Where shotguns are to be used for fox control, again almost any will do the job provided you are within range. For many years my preference has been for a semi-automatic 12-bore. Currently I use a Benelli Vinci. I have always liked this make, not only for its efficiency but also the engineering that goes into it, which is second to none. However, I started off with a Luigi Franchi before to a Browning five-shot. In later years I also had good service from a Beretta Al 591.

When the restriction of ownership of five-shot autos came in – and why this was ever been drafted I will never understand – I feared this would be a problem for me. In fact, I never really found that to be the case – for foxing, three shots should be more than enough. As I mentioned earlier, my choice of shot size has been BB for years. Particularly today when you can easily acquire three-inch and even three-and-a-half-inch cartridges in this shot size, a three-shot auto-loaded with anything up to 50-gram loads are more than good enough for foxes. If you have a shotgun that will handle these magnum cartridges, they will deal with a fox out to 50 yards or so – possibly further, but at these longer ranges there is always a good chance of the fox just being injured owing to the pattern being a little on the thin side.

There used to be a myth that provided you got a pellet or two into a fox, it would die quickly from lead poisoning. I fear that this is just not true, and that many foxes have been peppered at ridiculously long ranges by those who believe it. Having skinned many thousands of foxes over the years, I lost count of the number of foxes

and badgers (in the old days of course) that were carrying varying quantities of shot of all sizes and were perfectly healthy. Another point to remember is that foxes look bigger than they really are. Skinning a few soon makes you realise that, the odd big dog fox aside, there really isn't much to the average fox. When stripped of their pelt, with no brush and ignoring the long legs, there really isn't a lot left.

A word on reloading your own ammunition. For most of my shooting life, with the exception many years ago when I reloaded for my shotguns, I resisted going down the reloading route. As a fox controller I have never 'wasted'

ammunition shooting at targets, except for zeroing purposes, so I felt reloading was unnecessary.

In the end I gave in and set myself up with the necessary equipment to load for .22 Hornet and .223 Remington. So what, after all those years, did I think of reloading? Well, I have to say I enjoyed it, well I did after the initial numerous setbacks. These are part of the whole reloading package, I suspect, and you do sometimes wonder why you started. Then once you have mastered the basics, you expect it to be relatively plain sailing – but it isn't. Nevertheless, reloading is one of those activities that really gets a grip

Above: Mike gets some practice with a Revo 12-bore
Left: A variety of shotguns and rifles suitable for fox control

What did I deduce from all of this? Firstly, reloading can be good fun, and very therapeutic. Are the results better than what factory ammunition can produce? Yes, provided you have the ability, patience and cash to really go into it. Do you need that extra accuracy to shoot foxes? Not really. Is it cheaper than factory ammunition to load your own? In my case, no, though it really depends on what you do. I have little doubt that the target shooter who goes to the range regularly, trying out new loads and striving for perfection, does save money. For the average field shooter like me, it is cheaper to get factory ammo. There is not inconsiderable cost involved when you start out, and some of this cost is ongoing.

I suppose the way I would sum it up is that reloading almost becomes a pastime in its own right. As I have said, it is addictive, and I got considerable pleasure in shooting the first fox with my own load. I still really enjoy loading a few rounds, but for many fox shooters it would be cheaper to find a factory round that shoots satisfactorily in your rifle and stick to that.

People treat their rifles in many different ways. Some advocate cleaning after every outing; some hardly clean them at all. The problem today is that we all know rather too much. Magazines, websites and other media will all espouse their own points of view. When I started out, there was virtually no choice involved – you got what there was as post-war Britain wasn't producing or importing many firearms of any sort. The same applied to ammunition – you got what was available.

Few knew about velocities, twist rates, barrel lengths and so on. You simply went and got your rifle, then used it. Many today would find it surprising just how little we knew about the rifle side of the business. Even more surprising was the

on you, as you strive endlessly to improve your accuracy. You 'work up' new loads, endeavouring to get ammo that will group perfectly. In my case, it seldom did. Don't get me wrong – my loads did the job and I could shoot foxes with them, but like most loaders, I decided that was not enough. The groups had to be smaller, and smaller still. I bought more sophisticated equipment. I trawled the internet for tips; I spent increasing amounts of time and money.

fact that we shot considerable amounts of quarry. I have said elsewhere that today, even with all the wonderful equipment available to us, I don't shoot that much more than I did all those years ago. But had I had all the equipment back then, I would in all honesty have shot more than I did, as my fieldcraft skills were far and away superior to what they are today.

The rifles and shotguns we use for sport or business today are very sophisticated items, and in most cases you will not be disappointed with your gun, whatever you get. Most firearms are capable of performing to a level far above the ability of their owners. This is certainly the case with me!

NIGHT VISION AND THERMAL IMAGERS

Without a doubt the biggest change that has occurred in my many years of shooting at night has been the advent of night vision in its many forms. When I started going out at night after fox and rabbit, I never dreamed that there would come a day when you could leave the lamp at home, but see more than you could when you took it with you.

My own initiation into night vision happened, I suppose, about seven years ago. I had been speaking to a farmer friend, who told me that he knew someone who had some night vision equipment, and it was amazing. My ears pricked up at that piece of information, and I asked if it would be possible to see it in action. Eventually my friend got back to me saying the chap with the NV would be at the farm that very evening, and I would be more than welcome to come along.

There is always a sense of anticipation when you know you are going to see something that will probably amaze you, so it was with considerable excitement that I set off on a winter's evening. Needless to say, my expectations were extremely high.

I met the pair at the farm, introductions were made, and I was able to see the new wonder toy. It didn't look all that impressive, but the happy owner was clearly thrilled to bits with it, so after a quick drink we headed out into the night. I had taken my best lamp with me as back-up, but was told firmly that I mustn't under any circumstances shine it in the direction of the night vision unit when it was being used.

Leaning against the fence of one of the horse paddocks, my newfound friend peered into the night. After a few minutes said he could see a rabbit, and as it was basically pitch black I was more than impressed. After a running commentary on the rabbits' progress, the moment arrived, and the instrument was passed to me along with whispered information as to what to do. Peering into the night, I expected a wonderland of animals to appear, happily going about their lives and suffering no intrusion from extremely bright lights. Was that the picture that unrolled before my eager eyes? The answer to that question was a definite no. In truth I could see virtually nothing at all.

Passing this information back to the owner, I was told to find a white fence rail and follow that until I came to the third post, at the base of which was sitting a very helpful rabbit. Painstakingly following the instructions, I eventually located the base of the post, where I could see what I had seen before: nothing.

Another set of whispered instruction was sent my way, but with still no success,

Preliminary test of a night vision unit. This model is the front-mounted Pulsar DFA75

I passed the instrument back to the owner, who after a quick look muttered that the rabbit was still there. This time, after following the earlier instructions and arriving at the base of the post, I was asked in a fairly terse whisper if I could see a white blob. Yes, I said, I could, but where was the rabbit? That's the rabbit, he said. You're looking at its eye.

Feigning amazement, I apologised for my stupidity in not realising that what I had thought was a blob of paint on the post was, in fact, a rabbit's eye. We returned indoors to be regaled with stories of just how many rabbits had fallen while using this incredible invention.

That then was my introduction to night vision. I have no idea what make it was, but it goes without saying I didn't rush out the next day to spend my hard-earned cash on some night vision.

Time passed, and after a couple of years I began hearing reports of more night vision units coming into the country. More and more items on television showed pictures taken at night, and these looked amazing. Some digging around saw me trying out my first night vision binoculars from Deben. They were, compared with my first brush with NV, a revelation, and they were put into immediate use spotting both rabbits and foxes. They were first-generation binos and compared with today's items were really not that good, but they did show what was possible. Time passed and eventually I heard about the Archer 'add-on' monocular from Starlight NV in Manchester. A word to the ever-helpful owner Julian Marsh soon had an Archer on its way to me for a test.

It arrived, and after fitting it to the ocular lens of the scope on my Anschütz .22LR, I headed out with a farmer from the village to try it out. It wasn't quite the success I had hoped for, but it certainly caused my friend a great deal of merriment as I tried to see something recognisable through my scope. Returning home, I calmed down and started to play around with the settings of both the Archer and the scope. Soon I was getting hugely improved results, and was really thrilled at the obvious potential night vision held for the fox shooter.

A word of explanation might be appropriate here to anyone coming into the world of night vision for the first time. Referring to 'add-ons', they are units that you attach to your normal day scope, either on the front (objective lens) such as the Pulsar DFA75 or the rear (the ocular lens) such as the Archer. However, it is not a question of popping them on, heading out the door and shooting something. By using add-ons you clearly are altering the optics in your scope, and these need to be balanced with the optics in the night vision. I have had my Archer for several years now and it ranks among the very best of this type of unit, but it took quite some time before I was able to learn how to get the best out of it.

I have tried many types of add-on night vision equipment, and while this may be a generalisation, I have found the front-mounted types more difficult to set up than their rear-mounted counterparts. When using the rear types, you are using

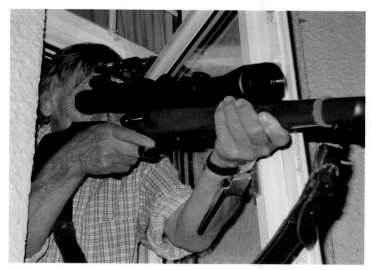

the scope's optics as they are meant to be used, but when using the front types, you are interfering with zero – it takes a lot more effort to overcome this. However, once this has been accomplished, they can perform almost on a par with the rear-mounted type.

I have used the Archer for years and it has served me well. Still available, it is still one of the very best night vision units you can buy; it can also be used as a handheld monocular, which I have done many times, using it to spot foxes and then switching to the lamp to finish the job. A word of warning, though: when using non-digital night vision units that have image intensifier tubes such as the Archer, Longbow and others, it is imperative that they are used only with infrared illuminators and not used at the same time as 'white light' or exposed to sunlight. This will damage the image intensifier tube.

There is another type of night vision scope, which can be used by day or night. Probably the best example of this is the Longbow, again from Starlight. This has what appears to be a conventional scope body but has interchangeable eyepieces,

The high life: Upstairs windows can make excellent and comfortable high seats

Home turf test: Mike after a fox in the back field at home

The digital NV system offers certain advantages over the conventional tubed night vision equipment we have become used to. Possibly the main one is that digital units cannot be damaged by bright light as the tubed versions can, meaning that the night vision unit can be used in daylight as well. This makes them far more convenient than tubed dedicated night sights. However, I would say that although they can be used in daylight and not damaged by it, they do present a very bright sight picture, so seeing a target in really sunny conditions is not too easy. You can get round this by zeroing late in the evening as the light starts to fade, or on an overcast day.

One of the first digital sights I tried was the Pulsar Digisight N550. At the time it was a pretty groundbreaking piece of equipment, and once you got your head around the zeroing instructions, it did a good job. This was followed by the N750, very similar to the N550 but with some improvements. These two systems are something of a technological landmark – they certainly allowed many more people to enter the world of night vision, as they were considerably cheaper than some of their predecessors.

So how did these newcomers perform? Once you got over the initial size and space-age appearance, they really were very good. Many claims were made as to their performance abilities ranging out to 600 yards or even more. In reality their abilities were less than that, although as far as I am concerned it's all academic, as I certainly don't shoot foxes at that range anyway. Where I found digital equipment really excelled was in the half-light as night fell. Under those conditions you could clearly see rabbits out to 400 yards, although again this is just an academic exercise.

It was clear that the digital age was really taking off. These two offerings from Pulsar

one of which is for normal day use and the other for when out at night. This scope can be zeroed and used in daylight in exactly the same way as a conventional scope in daylight, and will use exactly the same zero when the eyepieces are exchanged. The difference with the Longbow is that the scope body has been specially designed for the dedicated day-and-night units that fit by way of a bayonet fitting to the ocular end of the scope. This enables a far superior picture to be obtained at night, as there is no compromise by marrying one complete unit to another.

Of course, as with most things in life you get what you pay for, and this brings us nicely onto the digital revolution. I suppose in this world of miniaturisation – where mobile phones that not too many years ago were the size of a house brick are now getting smaller and smaller and store more and more information – it was inevitable that night vision would eventually go the same way.

were followed by, among others, the Pulsar DFA75. As mentioned earlier, this is a front-mounted device that fits over the objective lens of your existing day scope – in itself is a big advantage. However, there is always one problem that exists with front mounted add-ons and that is zeroing. The original instructions that were given with the DFA75 were, to put it mildly, challenging to follow, but various people put their minds to it and came up with some more accessible zeroing instructions. Leading this was *Sporting Rifle* magazine's Byron Pace, who did sterling work in putting together an easy-to-follow video. Once sorted, the unit performed well enough. This type of night vision is not my personal favourite, though there are many happy users out

there. I have found front-mounted add-ons are more likely to affect the balance of the rifle than the rear-mounted type.

Following hot on the heels of the DFA came the Yukon Photon. I was able to try one of the prototypes and was really impressed with it. It takes the form of a normal scope with a front end that could almost be taken for an add-on. However, it is made as one unit and is, for the money, one of the best digital buys available.

When I had the prototype I found it easy to set up – just like a conventional scope, in fact – and using it for the first time as the light faded, I was able to shoot rabbits with no problem out to 60 yards using my CZ 512 .22LR. As darkness fell it was perfectly usable out to 200 yards – perfectly adequate

the fields at night, they are almost a must-have item.

The thermal imager works by detecting infrared radiation given off by various objects – anything that has a higher heat range than the ambient temperature. So on a cold winter's night you will clearly see animals as well as such exciting things as dung heaps, as these clearly emit more heat than the surrounding environment. During the warmer summer months you will see other items such as tree trunks, walls and anything that absorbs heat.

The thermal camera 'reads' infrared emissions and then maps it to create an image. So what you see through your camera is a picture of heat radiation rather than a picture of the object itself. You will see that some creatures insulate themselves better against heat loss than others – wildfowl, for example, do not show as clear an image as, say, a chicken. That said, the picture any creature gives is easily good enough to recognise it by.

The range of thermal devices varies a bit, but my personal thoughts are that there is little need to recognise something 600 or 700 yards away, although it may be of passing interest. The exception to this would be the keeper, who would be more than interested in seeing what is going on in the fields he is responsible for.

Used in conjunction with good night vision unit mounted on your scope, with thermal imaging you have an extremely efficient means of controlling vermin over the land you shoot on. You can remain totally covert, still and quiet, and while it does not guarantee success, it certainly gives you an edge.

The question is often asked: What advantages does a thermal imager have over normal night vision? Well, as I said earlier, thermal imagers work on the infrared radiation emitted by any object, person or

for most shooters. As I write, the Photon retails at a fraction under £400.

The other big arrival on the night shooting scene has been the thermal imager. I have had experience of three of these: the Flir, the Guide and the Pulsar Quantum.

We have known about thermal imaging for a long time now, as they have been in military use for decades. But only recently have they been introduced to the civilian shooting market, and I have to say, they are amazing. Like top-of-the-range night vision, they are not cheap, and many will have difficulty justifying the expense just to shoot the odd fox or rabbit. However, for those who do a lot of night shooting and those whose livelihood takes them into animal. This enables them to work in total darkness – they do not require any ambient light to operate them at all. From a shooter's point of view it means that unless the target is obscured by something solid, no matter what the light situation may be ranging from daylight to total dark, the thermal imager will pick it up. So the fox walking behind a hedge will be seen as it passes gaps in it. Unlike conventional night vision, a thermal imager is not affected by hazy or foggy conditions.

Because the thermal imager works using the emitted heat from the target, even if the animal has its back to you or is only partially exposed, you will still see part of it, alerting you to the fact that something is there. Put simply, if it's there, you will see it.

Night vision scopes and add-ons such as the Longbow and Archer use image intensifiers. These work by amplifying the available light to enable you to see better. The objective lens focuses what light is available on to the photocathode of an image intensifier. Electrons are released from the cathode. Accelerated by an electric field and by using specially coated surfaces, which create more electrons, an electron 'cloud' is formed in the shape of the original image. This cloud hits a green phosphor screen, allowing the viewer to see the image. In other words, it does require an amount of light to work, as do digital NV units. This is provided by infrared, usually built in to the device or added on in the form of an infrared torch such as the Nightmaster. Good infrared is essential to get the best out of any night vision device.

With night vision, you are looking for the actual shape of the whole animal. If it has its back to you or is even partially obscured by foliage, it is unlikely you will see it. Most night vision users, myself included, rely heavily on picking up the reflection from night creatures' eyes. Should the eyes not be

looking in your direction, you aren't likely to pick it up.

Turning to the digital system, this works totally differently to standard night vision. The light comes through the objective lens of the unit, is processed through a charged coupling device (CCD), and is sent on to a liquid crystal display (LCD) where you can view the image. This type of night vision can be used in daylight, and its component parts are not affected by bright light. However, like the image intensifiers (even those using infrared add-ons), there will still be occasions where animals will not

Top: The DFA75 is a good example of a front-mounted unit... Above: ...but Mike tends to prefer rear-mounted types like the Archer, or dedicated NV scopes like the Yukon Photon (Image: Byron Pace)

Thermal imagers are fast becoming more accessible, and are one of the most effective night shooting aids there is. Image: Byron Pace

be seen, although this won't occur at the same frequency.

At the time of writing my preference is still for the image intensifier type, but the development of digital will, without doubt, improve rapidly. With their potential advantages I suspect the day may come when they will offer better results than the image intensifier types.

You may ask, "But what if spend a load of cash on one type, and the next day something better appears?" Look at it this way: you are buying something to let you shoot at a fox at night. My Longbow is a really brilliant piece of kit, and I have shot many foxes while using it. That won't change. Possibly in a few years there will be a digital device that will give a better picture than my Longbow. So what? My Longbow will still enable me to shoot a fox, and you can only shoot it once.

So what is the future of these various forms of equipment that allow us to see in the dark? As I said at the beginning of this chapter, what we have today was unheard of when I was a boy, so where we go from here is difficult to predict. Undoubtedly digital technology is the current new – and

very efficient – kid on the block. It is still in its infancy where shooting is concerned, but many of the leading firms in this field are improving and becoming more innovative all the time. So to answer my own question about what the future holds, all I can say is, "Wait and see."

Should you eventually take the plunge and decide to get yourself some night vision, my best advice is to try before you buy. This is not always possible, but as night vision use becomes more common, there should be more opportunities for you to get to know someone who will let you see what night vision is capable of. I have, for some time now, regularly had people round at my place to have a look at the various night vision devices I have. I think it's fair to say they have all found this a big help in deciding what to buy. Scott Country, one of the leading night vision suppliers, also started a loan scheme to allow prospective buyers to try the unit they are thinking of buying by letting them have it on loan on payment of a deposit.

So how do I use my night vision equipment? I am fortunate that I have some very nice equipment to use. Long divorced, and with all my children having left home, I only have myself to convince that I really need some product or other. Sadly I am very easy to convince, so over the years I have accumulated some very nice items, and doing the reviews I do for Sporting Rifle and Modern Gamekeeping has brought me in contact with many of the best makes on the market.

You can link conventional lamping with night vision, but I struggle to understand the way some people go about it. I have met several lampers who have some excellent night vision spotting aids, the Archer being one, but who use the lamp to pick up the fox's eyes in the first place and then use the night vision to try to get within range. This

Above: A fox taken with the aid of digital NV

seems backwards to me – putting the lamp on lets the fox know you are there when the whole purpose of night vision is the reverse.

If you use a high seat for foxing, which can be very successful, try the following tactic: spot your fox with the NV unit, call or just watch its progress, then when it is within range, switch to the lamp. Even very wary foxes can be dealt with using this method. Since they have no knowledge of your presence, when the light comes on they will, nine times out of ten, pause long enough for a shot to be taken.

If you wish to use this last method, there is one way you can improve on the spot-then-lamp system, and that is by using a red LED in your torchlight. I have a Nightmaster 800 fitted with one, and very effective it is too. It is infinitely better than a red filter fitted to a normal lamp. Foxes certainly don't seem to react anywhere near as much as they do with normal lighting. A torchlight fitted with a red LED also has the advantage that there is no leakage of white light – many normal lamps that have red filters fitted to them often leak white light around the rim or in other places. This will sometimes reflect back off your face or clothing – something the LED set up will never do.

The thermal imager linked with a good quality night scope is probably the pinnacle for covert fox control at present. The thermal device enables you to spot quarry out to ridiculously long distances – far greater than is practically necessary, but interesting when you are out at night.

The thermal imager presents just that, an image, so many ask how easy is it to identify the object you are watching. As with most things involved with wild animals, observation is the key here. When using thermal imagers it is not always possible to recognise exactly what the object registering on the screen is. But very quickly you get to identify species by movement and the way the object behaves. Possibly the biggest challenge is when suddenly in a field with 50-60 rabbits, a much larger object appears. The adrenalin starts pumping – this must be a fox. Suddenly your 'fox' splits into two pieces and you realise it was two rabbits overlapping. This happens quite often and you never quite get used to it.

That apart, you quickly pick out and recognise an animal by three key factors: size, the way it moves, and behaviour. Badgers have a rolling gait whereas the fox has a much daintier walk and trot, well up on its legs. Badgers spend a lot of time rooting about in a fairly restricted area, whereas the fox, although it will poke about, sometimes for quite long periods, it is not nearly as aggressive in its digging techniques. Badgers will frequently follow their traditional runs across a field in a purposeful way and at a steady gait; the fox will more often than not follow hedges and will proceed in a much more random fashion, stopping here and there as it catches wind of something. It may seem a bit strange at first, but once you know your equipment and set it up correctly, you will certainly not have any difficulty identifying the fox.

By spotting your fox and watching its progress, you can decide how best to deal with it. With a good night vision set-up you will soon note behavioural patterns that you never realised existed. Calling foxes is, and always has been, a very imprecise science – something you can witness for yourself when watching foxes through a thermal imager at night when they have no idea you are there. Many times I have watched, unseen, as foxes forage in a field, clearly hungry, and you switch on your digital caller with a speaker possibly 100 yards from you. What happens? Nothing. The fox doesn't even raise its head as a rabbit's scream splits the silence. It is totally ignored.

Hopefully, however, the fox will come in to a distance that makes an almost guaranteed shot possible, and at no time in the whole process have you revealed yourself. Using these modern, high-tech night vision aids will not only get you success if used properly – they will also increase your knowledge of the nation's top predator (after us, of course).

One point I would like to make is that although night vision in its various forms is becoming more and more affordable, much of it is still expensive. It is typical of us that we always like to keep up with the latest innovations and are prepared to pay to do so.

There are, and always will be, those less fortunate than some, for whom night vision may well be out of reach. I personally thoroughly enjoy using mine, and as I have said before it has opened up a whole new dimension to my shooting. However, I never lose sight of the fact that I have shot far more foxes without the aid of NV than I have with it. So if these modern wonders are beyond your reach, don't despair. The old methods will still work as well as they always have.

MY OWN FOXING EQUIPMENT

I am extremely fortunate to be in a position to test and review all sorts of items of clothing and equipment. Over the years, from the wide range of items I have come across, some have stood out as being ideal for my purposes.

I have to say, being more than a little advanced in years, I am inclined to go more for the practical type of gear than the gear that may be in fashion at the time. The choice of equipment available to the shooter today is bewildering in the extreme. When I started out, any old thing would do – the most common outfit was an old gabardine Mac and a pair of turned-down wellies. In fact most of us looked like Compo in Last of the Summer Wine.

Clothing is a case in point. There is an absolute plethora of clothing to choose from these days – much of it in camouflage patterns designed to make you invisible in conditions ranging from arctic snow, through desert sand, and winding up in an English marsh. Let's be clear: I have nothing against it whatsoever, and use some frequently. But personally, I still believe that the best camo design for general use in this country is the old military DPM.

This was brought home to me many years ago when out ferreting with Jim, who at that time had just left the military and had been recommended to me as a good bloke

with the ferrets. Jim, as it turned out, was a good bloke in every way, and over the years he has changed from a good bloke to a good friend. He is good with dogs, an excellent keeper, and totally proficient in all matters shooting. He is just the type to carry on the traditions of the countryside.

On the first occasion we went ferreting, Jim turned up wearing DPM. At some stage we were netting up some buries, I turned to see where he was, and couldn't see him. Eventually I spotted him lying in the hedge bottom, netting a particularly difficult bolt hole. He was almost invisible. In truth little of today's camo would work that well, although I would say that the quality of some of the larger brands is extremely good, with considerable thought going into design. I particularly like Rivers West Mossy Oak camo as it is quite dark, suiting the use I give it well – it is also very well made. The good old standbys of tweed and moleskin still work well for me too. I have used these for more years than I care to remember, and they still do the job.

I firmly believe that the best camouflage available is the way you move (or don't as the case maybe). Many times over the years I have had animals come really close to me, totally unaware of my presence. All I really did to achieve this was keep still, irrespective of what I was wearing.

The closest was a fox I called to within about three feet of me. It was a poultry killer and had to go. I only had the .22LR at the time. When it arrived I remained stock still, and when it turned to look back in the direction it had come from, I just reached out the rifle and put a shot behind its ear. Like many shooting people, I have had all sorts of creatures come within touching distance of me – deer, foxes, rabbits (these have actually run over me when I've been waiting for foxes) but every time that sort of thing happened, I was absolutely still.

Where modern clothing has improved immeasurably is in the comfort levels it offers. Most of the well-known makes are totally windproof, waterproof and silent.

Finally on the clothing front, I must mention an excellent lightweight, totally waterproof smock called the Cyclone, again from Rivers West. This is one of the most useful items I have come across – it folds away into its own pocket, is small and compact, and really is extremely good.

Next, footwear. Sadly I've always been a bit of a welly man. Again, being honest, it's much easier to slip into a pair of well-fitting wellingtons, especially as you get older, than to struggle with lacing up boots. That said, I have had some nice boots over the years. I rather like Seeland boots and have found some of the Dunlops pretty good too. On the leather front when keepering, both Le Chameau and Black Islander have

Night test: Mike in action with a Lightforce lamping set-up

The high seat is ideal for fox control in certain situations, but you do need patience

for a certain shot. If I am ever out waiting for fox, rabbit and occasionally pigeon, I always wear a veil, and more often than not gloves as well. Mind you, I don't walk around like that. There is no point – you will be seen whether you wear a veil or not when you are on the move. There is an added bonus during the summer months as a decent veil will keep off the midges.

Some of the equipment I have is only used occasionally when circumstances demand it. It's a bit like modern pigeon shooting – it's all too easy to end up with a truck full of gear, much of which is only useful once in a while.

One thing that has crossed over from my occasional pigeon shooting efforts is a camo net. Sometimes when preparing to wait for a fox, it is just not possible to get in a good spot to enable a safe shot to be taken; there may also be a total lack of natural cover. In situations like that I will sometimes make a very small hide – just a couple of poles and a lightweight net.

To get the best results I have found the best way is to put this up, if possible, a couple of days before you plan to use it. Foxes are very aware of their territory, and will sheer off anything that looks a bit out of place. Mind you, they can be curious. I once set up my 'mini hide', and upon returning to it to wait for a particular fox, found that one had beaten me to it and left a neat, unmistakable calling card inside the hide. I never got that fox – I think of that as a final gesture from one that got the better of me.

For many years now I have shot off sticks. I was never brilliant at free-standing shots, and as the years passed I was less and less inclined to get down and dirty in the prone position. It's all well and good in the summer, but at night in the depths of winter, in the mud and slime of fields where there were large flocks of sheep

served me well – the latter in particular stood up to some very hard wear.

Today, considerable sums are spent on some very nice clothing and footwear. Some, as I said earlier, is of excellent quality, but I wouldn't like to give the impression to newcomers to the sport that they need to spend an absolute fortune fitting themselves out from head to toe in the latest camo gear. There are more important things to spend your money on when starting out on your shooting life.

Along with the clothing I must mention face veils and gloves. Where the former is concerned, I have used one from Deben for years and wouldn't be without it. It surprises me how people dress up in expensive camo but leave their face and hands uncovered. Faces show up from considerable distances, and as most people are incapable of remaining dead still for prolonged periods, the sight of a white face bobbing about in the hedge will be spotted by a fox long before it gets close enough

or herds of cows, it just didn't appeal, so sticks it had to be. I tried monopods, bipods, tripods, quadrapods and even pentapods; in the end I always came back to the tripod, which I found gave a very steady platform to shoot from.

I tried pretty well every make there was, including the B&Q green garden cane type so many members of shooting forums sing the praises of. Two, however, have stood out from the rest, and these I use exclusively. The first is Viking Arms' Vanguard Quest, and the other is Seeland's Shooting Stick Lux, which I acquired from Scott Country. Both of these employ similar systems, and both are extremely sturdy in use.

Some find difficulty in deploying sticks quietly and quickly. I found with a bit of practice you could do both quite easily with my products of choice. As most of my shooting is done from static positions, the sticks can be set up ahead of time, and give a steady rest. Both have a swivelling u-shaped bracket on top, which I think is a must. The fixed-strap top type can be a real nuisance if you need to swing the rifle round to an acute angle. As I use a variety of rifles for foxes, I have printed out some ballistic range data for each rifle – this is taped on the rear stick. Totally unnecessary if you only use one calibre, but quite handy when you might be using anything from a .22LR up to a .223.

Mike in his keepering days, opting for the traditional greens over a camo pattern

Portable hides provide temporary cover, but need to be set up for a few days before use

I have collected quite a few fox calls and callers over the years, but I have to admit that the ones I usually have with me are the non-digital mouth-operated types. Some of the digital callers are very good at what they do, but as I have said elsewhere I have a feeling that the more naturally produced sounds have the edge over the mechanical types. I normally carry four calls on a lanyard round my neck. They are, in no particular order, the WAM, the Faulhaber Hen call, and a couple from he Best Fox Call, the Tenterfield type and the original black plastic mouth-organ type. All of these will work well on their day, are inexpensive, and providing you don't lose them, will last forever.

There is little to choose between the digital types as they all use similar recordings. The Fox Pro range is very good, with a wide selection of calls suited to this country. The Mini Colibri is a much smaller digital caller – I rather like this one simply because you can slip it in your pocket.

High seats have become something I use often these days, as I find for my selective control of foxes, waiting in a static position pays dividends. Most requests for fox control obviously come either from poultry or sheep owners, and more often than not there will be a suitable spot for placing one. At the time of writing there are a couple on the market that I have used: one I acquired from Bushwear, the other from Scott Country. The Bushwear model can be extended higher than the Scott Country model; they are both pretty portable and easy to assemble, which is essential. On occasions they can be handy for rabbit control as well.

As time passes, I find myself using my 4x4 more and more as a hide. I have said elsewhere that the modern fox is quite used to hearing, seeing and smelling vehicles, and more often than not it totally ignores them. In fact on more than one occasion when harvest is in full swing and at the end of the day farm machinery has been left out in the fields, foxes will inspect the various implements, showing no fear – only curiosity. So around poultry and similar situations where there are usually cars parked, one more won't make a lot of difference. Not to mention modern vehicles make really comfortable hides!

If you are setting up anywhere, be it in a hedge, behind camo netting strung on a couple of poles or in a high seat, always remember to watch your silhouette. So often I have seen people get ready to wait for a fox, particularly at ground level, and forget that from a fox's eye level, their head is plainly visible against the sky. Most animals recognise the shape of our heads as there isn't much else in nature that resembles the shape of a human head and shoulders, so always try to get something dark behind you, whether it is foliage or a building. Once again, I will stress: keep still!

Where night vision and thermal imaging are concerned, I have tried a

variety of makes and models and have settled on three that I use constantly. They are the Pulsar Quantum thermal imager, the Starlight Longbow day/night scope, and the Archer monocular. All the infrared required comes from the excellent Nightmaster 800 IR LED or its smaller counterpart, the NM200. These have served me well since they first appeared and do the job I required of them perfectly. But – and it's a big but – things are changing very fast. Digital night vision is developing rapidly, and without doubt much of the equipment in use today will in due course be superseded by improved models. If you are looking to enter the night vision world, it sometimes pays to look at the models that have been improved upon. Sometimes the improvements are cosmetic or comprise items 'added on' to the original. Perhaps the older model will be more than adequate for your use, and will also be less expensive.

Turning to my own rifles, I have four main fox rifles. First, for close work – out to 70 yards or so – and in confined or populated areas, an Anschütz 1717 .17 HMR, and a 1710 .22LR of the same make. For night shooting I have an Anschütz 17/70 .223, which is fitted with the Longbow. Finally I have the Steyr Classic, which I use for daylight shooting and when I am out

Kit in practice: A camo-clad Mike awaits another victim

with the lamp. I have found all these makes to be totally reliable and very accurate for the purposes I need. Clearly there are other makes that will do the job just as well, but having tried quite a lot of rifles, these are the ones I have settled for.

As far as ammunition is concerned, the Steyr likes Prvi Partisan and I reload for the Anschütz .223. Winchester ssubsonics are the usual fodder for the .22LR although it also likes CCI. I have always used Hornady in the .17 HMR and have never had a problem with it. Both the .223s will shoot most factory ammo perfectly well for the purpose I use them for with the exception of the Anschütz, which really doesn't like the Prvi offerings.

I personally think a rangefinder is absolutely essential for all forms of live quarry shooting. I really don't understand anyone leaving home to go shooting without one. They almost guarantee you getting better results with one than without. I have tried most makes from the cheapest to the dearest, and find that they all give very similar results when calculating distance, which is what I want one for. Some have a variety of extra facilities, but distance to the target is all I want. My own rangefinder is a Leica, which has the huge advantage from my point of view of having an illuminated readout.

I now arrive at what can be a slightly contentious issue: optics. Under that heading come scopes and binoculars. As you will know whether you are a beginner or someone who has shot for years, the choice is bewildering to say the least. Starting with the binoculars, if you are seriously after foxes (or any other quarry for that matter), a good pair is almost a necessity. The problem arises when you try to decide which pair to get. It seems everyone has their own opinion as to which is the best, and they won't hesitate to share it with you.

That's fair enough, as one person's vision can be very different from another's. I have a feeling too, though it's only based on anecdotal evidence, that with optics there seems to be a bit of one-upmanship. To be fair there are a great many makes out there to choose from, some of them undoubtedly better than others, but whether you need to pay thousands rather than hundreds can be a moot point.

Some years ago I did a comparative test on many of the well-known makes. Typical of me, it was practical rather than technical – in other words, did they do the job I wanted them to do? My test consisted of putting a dark-coloured, fox-sized log in a sheltered corner of the field across the valley from my home. From midday until dark I tried them all (there were, I think, about six or seven makes) every quarter of an hour to see which could pick out the log best.

During the really bright part of the day there was precious little between them, but as the light started to fail, differences appeared. To bring a long and not very exciting story to an end, the final results were surprising. The best result overall, taking price into consideration, was from a pair of Minox 7x42s, and this is the make and magnification I use myself along with

Above: The days of lying in mud are long gone – Mike has shot off tripods for years
Left: Portable high seats can be a good shooting solution

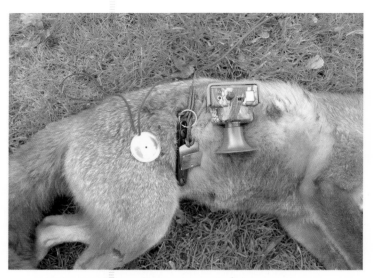

a pair of Hawke Frontier 8x36 binos. Both of these do everything I require of them and don't break the bank.

There are other top makes, of course, and I can't go any further without mentioning Swarovski. Their optics are extraordinarily good – they are almost impossible to fault. Were I a bird watcher or wanted a pair of binos to use at home and had the money, this is the make I would go for. But for foxing where there can be a bit of 'rough and tumble' with the elements and obstacles, I feel that with such a top-end pair of binos with me, I would be more worried about keeping the binoculars safe than achieving the job in hand!

Staying with optics, we now arrive at something that probably raises more arguments and discussion as anything else in shooting. Almost everyone has their views on almost every aspect of the telescopic sight. What is the best magnification? And should that be variable or fixed? Do you need an illuminated reticle? Should you pay thousands, or next to nothing? The arguments go on and on.

Certainly as far as rimfires are concerned, I honestly think the debate has been exaggerated, and it matters a lot less than you think. Apart from the really downmarket efforts, most scopes will perform well enough at the ranges you are likely to use this type of rifle at.

On my fairly upmarket Anschütz 1710 .22LR I have mounted a Hawke Eclipse scope with a MAP8 reticle. This combination has accounted for thousands of rabbits and more than a few foxes, and the scope, I seem to remember, cost less than £100. My .17 HMR has a Leupold mounted on it, a middle-priced scope that I have a high regard for. This rifle is used a lot at night where better optics are an advantage.

My .223 for daylight use has a Swarovski Z6i 3-18x50 mounted on it. This is an extremely good scope, and in truth it is the best piece of optical equipment I have. Again I wouldn't say it is necessary for general shooting – nice, but not necessary. For foxing, though, when the fox more often than not shows itself just as the light fails, it is ideal.

Along with the Swarovski, Leupold and Hawke scopes, I would add MTC as a brand that offers very good value for money. The only advice I can offer to anyone looking for a scope would be to set yourself a price ceiling and look at those scopes available at that level. Whatever you get, it is unlikely you will be disappointed. I doubt that the average shooter will shoot much more

using a £2,000 scope than he would using a £500 model.

My lamping equipment comprises a Deben lithium ion battery linked to a Tracer Sport Light 75-watt halogen lamp. Both are from Deben, and are both very light and effective. Years ago I also used Lightforce equipment, and like many others I found them more than fit for purpose.

While it is not strictly for foxing, when I am out after rabbits I use the excellent Jetbeam BC40 with white LED. I chose this make from among a crowded market as it not only has a very tight spot, it also throws a good 'halo' around the spot. Both perfect, and essential, for lamping rabbits. However, if using a lamp in conjunction with night vision, I normally go for the Nightmaster 800 with red LED. As I wrote elsewhere, the LED has taken us forward from the filter method we used for so long. I have never been a fan of filtered red light for night shooting, whatever the quarry may be, as a red filter considerably reduces the lamp's range. The LED has changed that, allowing a change of coloured light at night – red, blue, amber and increasingly, green to be used at realistic distances. One final lamp

Above: A stealth camera catches a glimpse of Charlie Left: The variety of calls on the market is astounding. Some work; some don't

All this kit just to shoot a fox! But there's no doubt it makes foxing easier when used right

that I use is the 4Greer Nightmaster, from Inovatech, a quality lamp throwing a tight, long-distance (400 yards) beam – ideal for some forms of foxing.

I use trail cameras quite a lot as they can reveal a great deal of information, particularly when first setting out after a problem fox. They tell you exactly what wildlife is about at night, and provide what can be vital information as to which direction the offender comes from. Apart from that, they can be set up for continuous surveillance, which can be very revealing. I must admit that using them can become quite addictive – most mornings my first job is to check out what has been about in the back field.

My own choices are Minox or Spypoint. There are, however, many other makes on the market that I am sure will do the job. Like most of this type of equipment, it will come with several facilities you will possibly never need. They can be a bit strange to set up to start with, but with practice you will find a trail cam not only a very useful item of equipment, but also good fun.

These are the tools of my trade. There are a very wide range of all these pieces of equipment available, and I wouldn't like you to think I have tried or tested all of them – nowhere near. For anyone coming into this area of shooting, my advice, as always, is: try as many as you can and make up your own mind.

LOOKING BACK, LOOKING FORWARD

As I draw near the end of the story of my long life involved with the fox, what are my thoughts? I have tried hard to set out things as they were, and in some cases still are. Clearly much has changed. Most shooters of my generation started off as loners, as I did, and apart from the odd friend who shared my love of the countryside, most have gone. We saw and lived through times that in some cases changed the world forever – in particular the war. The male population after hostilities ceased was greatly reduced, and no more so than out in the country. This left a void, which those of my generation slowly started to fill.

While that was happening, there was a general feeling in the countryside of live and let live. I, and probably many others like me, did not have the difficulties people do today in finding land to shoot over. In fact in my own case, through a mixture of effort, my location, and having good friends in the farming community, this has never been a problem. In that, I count myself extremely fortunate.

Things were also different in that there was nowhere near the violence, thieving and general mayhem that runs through society today. Particularly in the rural areas, everyone knew everyone else, so the occasional 'bad lot' was soon sorted.

There was a freedom where gun and rifle ownership was concerned that those starting off in the shooting sports arena today can only wonder at. I can remember as a lad in my teens going into the local post office to renew my gun licence, which I seem to remember cost 50p in present day money. I just went in, and headed out on my way to some nearby land, my trusty old hammer 12-bore tucked under my arm. No one gave me a second glance.

There would have been a slightly different reaction today, I suspect. At present country sports of all types are under considerable threat from those who, for one reason or another, are against them. I have watched this develop for years. It started with the outcry against the breeding of animals for their skins. This was swiftly followed by people campaigning against wild animal fur of any sort being used for the pleasure of humans. Where the fox was concerned, all it did was end many people's livelihood, and to what purpose? It certainly didn't stop foxes being killed – all it did was ensure what was a useful by-product became useless overnight. So the attractive and useful pelt was dumped or buried, a practice that continues to this day. What a waste.

Eventually the Hunting Act was passed – a shameful and utterly pointless piece of

legislation if ever I saw one. Unworkable, costly and again doing nothing to protect a species that in all honesty is pretty well equipped to look after itself, it was again an intrusion into the workings of a countryside that had managed itself pretty well for a very long time indeed.

To think that it is possible to, at a stroke, give a species – as in the case of the badger – total protection and not expect dire consequences is naïve in the extreme. There was a time when I shot badgers for their skins. Anyone who had problems with

badgers could handle the matter as they saw fit. Did it affect the badger population? Not at all – there were always plenty around, but numbers were kept at sensible levels and until the ban on killing badgers, bovine tuberculosis was also kept under control.

The fox has always been a prime target for the countryman and keeper, and as a wily and not unintelligent creature, his path has always been inextricably entwined with that of man. It is interesting to look back at how people view the fox today compared with back then. If a group

of villagers met in the pub, at some stage of the proceedings there would almost always be some mention of foxes. Either along the lines of "I saw a big dog fox crossing the front meadow today" (big foxes are always dogs and small foxes vixens – a popular misconception that is still heard today), or "That vixen with the limp is still hanging round my chickens," and the discussion would go on from there.

A couple of times a year the hunt would meet in the village. Pretty much everyone would turn out for the occasion. All the local experts were out, and there was much banter. The talk quite naturally was of foxes, hounds, horses and the like – it was a bit like harvest supper, when the whole village would unite. At the meet there would be much talk of where foxes had been seen and what fine specimens they were. Almost everyone would be chatting to the Master and the hunt servants, espousing their own views as to how the hunt should go.

Foxes were referred to as "our" foxes, and everyone talked about how they would be

A few things to spend your money on... Foxing kit has changed irrevocably over the years

The vixen on her way back to the cubs after a bit of scavenging

sure to give the hounds a good workout. This rather proprietary approach was in somewhat stark contrast to just a day or two later, when things returned to normal and it was back to "That bloody old lanky dog fox has been after Frank's chickens again," or the rather more positive "I'll shoot the bloody thing if it comes near my birds." Sadly, with the increase in traffic on the main road between the village and the cliffs where many of the hunted foxes would head to, the hunt eventually found

it too hazardous to hunt this area anymore. Yet another part of village life disappeared, never to return.

Another change came about with the tightening of firearm legislation. In the past most interested parties in the village kept a gun behind the door ready for action, and this way many a fox was dealt with after the dogs gave warning. Now, by the time you have found the keys to the cabinet, got the gun out very carefully so as not to mark the woodwork, found the cartridges,

loaded the gun and got outside, all you will probably find are a few feathers. Charlie will be on his way with yet another victim, and you will have to tend to the injured.

The behaviour of the fox has changed in my lifetime. Years ago foxes would generally only visit human habitation when hunger or the need to feed cubs forced them to. Today, even leaving the town fox out of the equation, foxes seem to have little fear of humans – and in truth, why should they? I can only speak from my own experience in the village I have lived in for the greater part of my life. Here it is now common to see foxes, and with the introduction of stealth cameras you soon come to realise that there are foxes around our property after dark on a nightly basis.

The very fact that they now interact with us has changed some aspects of their behaviour. When I first started out, lights were rarely seen a couple of hours after dark. Now they are everywhere – security lights, car lights, house lights, dogs, people,

The dead fox in the field was taken with the Anschütz .17 HMR at 70 yards

Above: The results of two different, but equally devastating, fox attacks

imaging and highly sophisticated night vision to see where our quarry is without it knowing we are there at all. Rifles in the right hands, as I said earlier, have largely taken the place of shotguns, and the lamps of all types that are now available would completely blow away the old ones we cobbled up. Today we think nothing of jumping into our 4x4 vehicles and going off-road in search of our quarry. Even ferreting has become infinitely easier, as I can drive to where we will be working and take a load of equipment with us with no difficulty at all. This is in stark contrast to my early days when there was absolutely no transport available, except perhaps a pushbike, and we would walk up to three miles to our rabbiting permission and then walk back carrying a load of rabbits. Good old days!

So where does all this leave the rural fox? What does the future hold for this creature, which has been part of the British countryside for centuries? Clearly it has adapted to the ever-changing world of the human, and presumably it will continue to do so. In all, I think those who shoot are more likely to have more problems that the creatures they shoot at. There is increasing political and social pressure on shooting sports of all persuasions. The anti-shooting lobby appears to be gaining strength, and in a rather more cohesive way than those who would protect the sport.

I don't think that those starting off on their shooting lives today realise just how much legislation, both in force and proposed, has appeared in only the last 30 years or so. Much of this has been triggered by a few tragic incidents, which have little or nothing to do with most sensible, law-abiding gun owners. From what I see and hear, the streets of the country are awash with illegally held firearms, but sadly and increasingly, guns of all sorts are coming

all of which can be found everywhere up to midnight and often later. If it sees these things on a nightly basis, and most of them do it absolutely no harm, is there is any reason for a fox to be unduly nervous?

I always go on about the lack of knowledge of fieldcraft today, but sometimes I wonder if the need for it is as great as it was. We had to learn to tread quietly, to move through the night almost silently; today we have thermal

Retrieval: Talon in his prime years

under attack irrespective of who the owners may be.

There has also been a proliferation in the number of bodies representing the shooting fraternity in recent years – but proliferation does not guarantee strength. As with most organisations, they tend to be focused in the direction of their own members and their particular interests. In a way, this is quite understandable. I don't find it surprising that clay shooters, for example, are not generally too interested in the problems of the deer stalker – and vice versa. The percentage of shooters in the community overall is really rather small. But if we were all under one umbrella, we could make quite a loud noise. The antis do it – why can't we? The problem is that any amalgamation would mean job losses, so I doubt it will ever happen.

Returning to how all this may or may not affect the subject of this book, the fox, I suspect he will go on much as before. I am not sure how the hunting ban affected fox numbers, but I would guess that they are pretty much as they have always been. Increasing road traffic probably accounts for the bulk of non-natural fox deaths. Robert Bucknell, in his first book *Foxing with Lamp and Rifle*, which I consider to be absolute essential reading for anyone interested in foxes, puts the

Poultry marauder: Another fox caught in the act

over, which I would say has certainly not enhanced the situation generally. There are quite a lot of scattered areas of woodland, thick hedges and undisturbed areas. Half a mile away is an RSPB reserve on the cliff land, dedicated to the preservation of the cirl bunting. For the purposes of my fox population guesstimate, let's say the total extent of the cliff frontage amounts to about a mile and a half.

All in all this area could be described as ideal fox country, and last year I decided to try and get an idea of the foxes that lived in and around the parish. I had my newly acquired thermal imager, and I also had more or less total freedom to roam the area at will. I had done a similar exercise a few years back and wondered how the two would compare.

Despite foul weather threatening to put me off, I decided the best way would be to ascertain the numbers of active breeding earths, the numbers of cubs, and if possible the number of non-breeding adults. Locals who could be relied upon to give accurate information on fox movements were involved, as were all the local farmers and smallholders. I would follow up reports of sightings; I was out most days and a lot of nights with the thermal imager, checking on the situation myself. The biggest problem I encountered was 'overlap'. Clearly several people would see the same fox, so as far as was possible I tried to get descriptions of those seen.

As the extraordinarily wet summer moved on, a far clearer picture began to emerge as to the breeding situation of the local foxes. There were, of course, several barren vixens and free-ranging dog foxes, and there would always be a bit of a question mark over just how many of those there were. As far as the breeding sites were concerned, there were more than I had originally thought. I don't think for a moment that anywhere near all

fox population at around 240,000, with an expected reproduction figure per year of around 400,000. That it what we have to strike a balance with. However, since Robert's book was published I suspect the figures may have changed. Hunt kills (14,000 in 1998) clearly no longer apply. It is extremely difficult to guess accurately what the fox population overall may be.

In my own case I have tried to ascertain, as accurately as possible, what the fox population is in my own parish, which I know very well indeed. It comprises 2,250 acres, and the population is about 650. There is a central village with three or four outlying hamlets. The land is very hilly and a variety of farming is carried on, but with the changes in farming, the dairy side of the industry has disappeared in the last 20 years and has been largely replaced with beef production, cereals, a small amount of market gardening, some sheep and free-range poultry. Many small parcels of land have been sold, and the horse fraternity has taken these

of them were found, especially out on the cliffs where it would be totally impossible to check and even find all of them. However, nights spent with the thermal imager revealed regular adult movements, which suggested there was a breeding earth in that vicinity.

In the end I reckoned there were somewhere in the region of 35 active earths. Among the ones I was able to watch and count the cubs, the number of young at first emergence ranged from three to six. The summer, as previously mentioned, was truly horrendous, which certainly affected the local rabbit population, and as a direct result the number of cubs reaching maturity must have been less than normal – although I have to say the earths I was watching seemed to manage perfectly well.

As the cubs matured and left the earths, it became more and more difficult to recognise the various families, and so I based my somewhat random survey on the time when the cubs were about ready to leave the earth. I estimated that the number of cubs setting out to hunt with the vixen averaged at four, so at that stage the local fox population would have been around 140 cubs plus 70 adults plus the barren vixens and solitary dog foxes – all adding up to a staggering 230 foxes.

Out and about: Mike has been surveying foxes on his home patch for 50 years

Foxing team: Talon is the most versatile dog Mike has owned

Of course, this number would immediately start to drop when the cubs left the earths, as they would be vulnerable to road deaths and other causes, and I know for a fact that several of the old foxes disappeared along the way too. So my final best guess would be there were around 200 foxes going into the winter, which struck me as a lot. It also struck me that this was the reason I am kept so busy endeavouring to keep numbers under control.

Mange is always a problem in this area, and I would think this unpleasant affliction accounts for the death of many foxes infested with the mite. I also noted that in a couple of the earths, either the vixen or the dog showed signs of mange, which would undoubtedly be passed on to their offspring.

I, along with the odd other person who shoots a few foxes, account for somewhere around 100 foxes a year in the parish, so with natural and accidental deaths counteracted to a degree by newcomers drifting in to the area, I suspect the number of foxes going into the next year's breeding system will be roughly the same as the previous ones. There must be a considerable number of fox deaths that go unnoticed, and it is that sort of event that makes accurate recording difficult. Some surveys work on faecal counts taken over a large area. I have no idea how accurate this method must be – all I can say is that either the foxes that are local to me must be either starving or suffering from severe constipation. I am out and about over the same areas constantly, though I don't exactly spend time looking for fox droppings, I don't miss much and I don't see that many.

I found my unscientific survey a very interesting exercise, and I did get to know where the foxes are. Various little things showed up that were of interest. There was one occurrence of very young cubs being killed, probably by a lone dog fox (I have come across that before). Also at times there would be chance meetings between what were clearly members of the same family group and at other times between rival factions. Areas travelled by certain foxes varied enormously, as did the times normal (not cub-feeding) hunting took place.

During this exercise I did learn much about the fox that I hadn't been aware of before – so from that point of view it was a success. I don't think for a moment that I'd found every single earth, or that all the litters reached maturity. Tracing behaviour patterns of individual foxes is hard enough; tracking the whole population of the parish can at best result in a rough guide to the situation. All I know is that when you really look into the matter, there are a lot more foxes out there than we are aware of.

As to the future, as far as the fox is concerned I doubt that very much will change, for the wild country fox at least. He has survived many things over the many years he has been involved with man. He has been sought after, protected when hunting was the norm, and persecuted for his misdeeds since time immemorial. Various afflictions come

and go and reduce his numbers, but still he survives and in many areas thrives. His relationship with humankind changes as time passes, and I suspect the fox now has more friends than foes. Certainly in the countryside the attitude towards Reynard has changed in my lifetime. No longer are most hands turned against this expert predator. As more people move to a 'green' way of living and try their hands at keeping their own poultry and looking to live in harmony with the wildlife, so the fox gathers more friends. At least until he shows his true colours and kills their chickens. That seems to change attitudes remarkably rapidly.

There are now vast amounts of money poured into the countryside to promote wild places and encourage wildlife – all excellent news for the fox. Much of the land I have roamed over for most of my life now has more rough areas and scrub than ever before – again, all good for the fox. In my area, and I guess in many other parts of the country as well, more large tracts of land are being split up and sold off to eager newcomers, who generally let it go back or put up stable blocks, all of which provide rich pickings and shelter for foxes. Although more people are going out endeavouring to shoot foxes than ever before, I suspect the yearly total killed is gradually dropping as the number of professional fox men diminishes. So as far as I can see, the wild fox's future looks pretty rosy.

I suspect the urban fox will not be so fortunate. Many in our towns and cities are becoming exasperated at the ever-increasing numbers of foxes roaming their streets. There have been well-documented cases of fox attacks on children and pets, and while our town brethren say how wonderful it is to see wild creatures in the street, this romantic approach soon

turns sour when such events as mentioned above take place.

Many and various are the TV programmes devoted to urban foxes, many of them glamorising the animal. Those who really do know foxes soon see the problems, such as the increasing prevalence of mange. I understand there have been many cases of domestic animals picking up this distressing affliction, again not endearing the town fox to the local populace. Then there is mating time – for the foxes, not the populace. The screams of romance are all well and good where they are meant to be, in the open field and hill of the countryside, but certainly not in the confines of an urban cul-de-sac.

I know from friends I have who live in such situations and who once were really excited to report the siting of a fox in their garden. After some experience of *Vulpes vulpes*, they have totally changed their outlook – in fact on more than one occasion I have been asked if I could take a trip to town and sort a few out. Sadly I suspect King Canute endeavouring to sweep the tide out would have more success than me trying to stem the tide of vulpine infestation. Unless there is a severe outbreak of mange that decimates the urban fox population, my guess is that there will soon be official moves taken to severely reduce the number of foxes in our towns and cities.

Of course we know many of these animals are caught and deposited in the countryside. Many will survive and adapt, as adaptation is something the fox is very good at. There is a train of thought by many in the country that these dumped foxes invariably succumb to the rigours of rural life. This is certainly true in many cases, but I have a feeling the biggest cause of death is those who come across them and shoot them in the early days after

The result of a successful outing with the H-S Precision .243

release. While I understand they are in a new environment, so tuned are their senses to seek out food that I very much doubt they will starve. They will eat virtually anything if pushed, and their noses will soon sort out a new diet for them.

So certainly for the foreseeable future, the fox will not only survive but will thrive. They are probably our most adaptable large mammal and have learned how to live alongside man, if not in total harmony, for much of the time.

Foxes are certainly not unintelligent creatures – without doubt they have learned from their centuries of contact with man how to exploit his weaknesses. I have taken the lives of countless foxes over my time, but have always had a high regard for them. At times they have caused me grief when they have turned their attentions to my pheasants or poultry, and on countless occasions I have seen the total carnage they can cause and the attendant upset and cost it can bring. But as I have said elsewhere, we are not so different. We need to exercise control over the humans who transgress certain aspects of our lives; so, too, do we need to control the fox.

My life since a very early age has always been involved with this country's top predator, the fox. I have spent vast amounts of time pursuing it for gain, but also just watching it. In some cases where the former was concerned, it has outwitted me; in the second it has given me much pleasure just observing it go about its business. It is a fascinating creature that probably divides opinion more than any other of our native species.

The emotions I have experienced over the years as far as the fox has been concerned have ranged from outrage, through frustration, to admiration. I wouldn't have missed a minute of it.

A FOXING LIFE WITH GUN AND RIFLE

ACKNOWLEDGEMENTS

Many thanks to all at Blaze Publishing for their help and guidance, in particular Colin Fallon for his patience and assistance at all times and Pete Carr who has been unfailingly supportive and helpful.

Charlie Jacoby who instigated my return to writing and again has always been there to offer his expertise.

Judy Marchant for her help in producing excellent photographs, not only for this book but for many of my articles, and for proofreading the original copy.

Brian Phipps for his long-time help on matters photographic and for allowing his highly professional photos to be used.

To my many farming friends over the years, in particular David and Peter French, Frank, Sally and Jeremy Saunders, and all the others who have allowed me the privilege of having unrestricted access to their land.

To Russell and Anne Dennis for the happy memories of keepering years.

To all the keepers I have known, some no longer with us.

Keeper Smith, George House, Alan Easterbrook, Geoff Cook, Ian Brown and Howard Green.

To my shooting friends stretching back over so many years, Johnny Pugh, Charlie Steere, Maurice Wallis, Pete Pinson, Robbie Austin and particularly Jim Parker. Good friends all.

Finally to the fair countryside of Devon and its foxes. It is impossible to quantify just how much both have given me.

INDEX

ABOUT THE AUTHOR

At the end of the Second World War at the age of eight, Mike and his parents moved from Wembley to Teignmouth in Devon. Education followed at Brook Hill Primary, ending up at the local grammar school.

Early days were spent roaming the fields with an air rifle, or fishing from a little rowing dinghy in the river Teign or out at sea. Shooting predominated, however, starting a lifelong connection with guns, foxes, ferrets and rabbiting. Together with a school mate Johnny, he spent hours after rabbits, foxes and pretty much everything else.

Time passed and National Service intervened. Eventually family pressures meant a steady income was needed, and he spent a few years with the Prudential, finally joining the NFU. Both jobs allowed him to spend much time after foxes and rabbits.

Early retirement at the age of 50 meant Mike was able to follow his passion for shooting, and the next 25 years were spent on keepering, beekeeping and other projects – and, of course, fox control. Finally retiring from keepering a couple of years ago, he now spends time writing on the subjects that have always been part of his life: foxing and rabbiting. He is a member of the Devon and Cornwall firearms licensing committee, but most of his time is spent, as it always has been, in the Devon countryside.

Twice married with three sons and a daughter, Mike now lives in the village that has been home for over 40 years with his dog and his ferrets.